Vegan Junk Food

No Meat, No Dairy, Lots of Love!

Junk Food

225 SINFUL SNACKS THAT ARE GOOD FOR THE SOUL

LANE GOLD

Adamsmedia

Avon, Massachusetts

Published by
Adams Media, a division of F+W Media, Inc.
57 Littlefield Street, Avon, MA 02322. U.S.A.
www.adamsmedia.com

ISBN 10: 1-4405-2897-7
ISBN 13: 978-1-4405-2897-2
eISBN 10: 1-4405-2986-8
eISBN 13: 978-1-4405-2986-3

Printed in the United States of America.

10   9   8   7   6   5   4   3   2

Library of Congress Cataloging-in-Publication Data
is available from the publisher.

This publication is designed to provide accurate and authoritative information with regard to the subject matter covered. It is sold with the understanding that the publisher is not engaged in rendering legal, accounting, or other professional advice. If legal advice or other expert assistance is required, the services of a competent professional person should be sought.
—From a *Declaration of Principles* jointly adopted by a Committee of the American Bar Association and a Committee of Publishers and Associations

Many of the designations used by manufacturers and sellers to distinguish their product are claimed as trademarks. Where those designations appear in this book and Adams Media was aware of a trademark claim, the designations have been printed with initial capital letters.

This book is available at quantity discounts for bulk purchases.
For information, please call 1-800-289-0963.

Dedication

To Josh, Jaide, and Ethan for inspiring me to cook.
And to Jason for being you.

Acknowledgments

My most sincere gratitude to Julie Chadwick for making this cookbook possible and for all the vegan potlucks. A very special thanks to Wendy Simard for making sense of all of this and for being so generous with her talent. A huge shout-out to my cooking compañeras Rosa Romero, Tanya Selig, and Suzy Martinez. To Shelly Brown for reminding me that this and all things should be fun! Last but not least, I thank my mom and extended family for giving me many kitchens full of love, patience, and encouragement.

Contents

Chapter 2—Deli Favorites: Sandwiches, Wraps, Burgers, and Sliders . . . 27

Chapter 3—Comfort Food Meets Takeout: Tempting No-Meat Entrées . . . 49

Chapter 4—Crusts and Carbs: Pizza Pies and Badass Breads . . . 75

Chapter 5—Festive Grub: Vegan Party Essentials . . . 97

Chapter 6—Dips for All Seasons . . . and All Reasons . . . 119

Chapter 7—Savory Treats: With a Touch of Sugar and Spice . . . 135

Chapter 8—Cakewalk (Pies, Too): Who Needs Butter? . . . 143

Chapter 9—Candy and Cookie Fix: For the Ultimate Sweet Tooth . . . 169

Chapter 10—Grab 'n' Go Sweets: Sinful Bars, Brownies, and More . . . 193

Vegans Just Want to Have Fun (Food), Too

I don't know about you, but I suffer from snack attacks and midnight munchies. Sometimes I like my dinner deep-fried, and on occasion I've been known to eat dessert first. And I know I'm not alone. Whether you're a vegan, raw foodie, pescatarian, or strictly a meat-and-potatoes type, nothing appeals to our collective cravings more than tried-and-true junk food.

Unfortunately, vegan options for these soul-comforting goodies can be woefully lacking! I can't tell you how many times I've read the label and had to put that delicious-looking box of cookies back on the shelf. Through my work feeding the vegan community, I've found many of us are in the same boat: We feel left out while reading menus at popular restaurants, and that's just the beginning. Delivery pizza? Forget it. Holiday parties? Hope you like carrot sticks. Taco stands? Keep walking. Bakery windows full of cakes? Looks decadent, but sadly, not for us.

Well, now would be the time to wipe your tears because there's a vegan way around even our most gnarly snack conundrums. As a vegan for a decade and a personal chef for five years, I've listened closely to my cravings and come up with creative ways to quell these hunger pangs using conscientious food choices. Until now, no book compiled junky recipes that are also animal-friendly and gentle on the planet (and by "junky," I mean sinfully delicious!). With 225 mouthwatering recipes that span from savory to sweet and many that mix the two, there's no shortage of new goodies here for you to test out and enjoy. With the right recipe, you can turn black beans and caramelized onions into gourmet burgers, and make kale taste like nacho chips. Inside you'll find a junk food fix for anything you fancy:

* **Craving chocolate?** Whip up a batch of Chocolate Chunk Brownies (see "Grab 'n' Go Sweets").
* **Hankering for a hot dog?** How about Corn Dogs with a Tangy Mustard Dipping Sauce (see "Comfort Food Meets Takeout").
* **Pining for pizza?** There are a baker's dozen of options inside, ranging from the straightforward Spicy Onion and Sausage to the truly exotic Tandoori Tempeh Pizza (see "Crusts and Carbs").

As food manufacturers are beginning to heed the demand for vegan staples, it's becoming easier to find vegan versions of common ingredients used in recipes. (See "VeganEssentials" for some of my favorite brands.) Modifying some recipes merely entails subbing an ingredient like butter with vegan margarine, while other recipes entirely recreate classics, like Eggplant Bacon (see "Breakfast of Champions"), that taste like the real deal. In yet other recipes, you can use what People for the Ethical Treatment of Animals (PETA) calls an "accidentally vegan" snack like Oreos and transform them into a dessert that ends up being even more sublime.

In the end, I've learned that we can still be addicted to ice cream; we just need to make it in our own kitchens. And I'm thrilled to be able to show you how. So stock your pantry and scratch that itch. Succumb to your sweet tooth or your craving for crunch—and know that you're in very good company.

— Lane

P.S. Unlike other vegan books, here you won't find quotations around animal foods like meatball, cheese, egg, ice cream, etc. That's because the whole book would be littered with them! Just rest assured that every recipe you find here is appropriately vegan—and in most cases, even more flavorful than the original.

VeganEssentials

In order to veganize nonvegan goodies, you need to become familiar with a whole host of ingredients that'll become your best allies in the kitchen. Here's a guide to the animal-friendly pantry items that help make your junk food taste oh-so-good. Many of these items can be purchased online at VeganEssentials (*www.veganessentials.com*).

NONDAIRY MILK

For recipes in this book that specify using nondairy milk, any of the following unsweetened milks will work: almond milk, hemp milk, rice milk, coconut milk, or soymilk. Choose the one you prefer to drink. When soymilk is specifically listed as an ingredient, it is usually for the body that it lends to the finished product; rice milk tends to be a little more watery. Replace soymilk in a recipe with a milk equal in body such as hemp or almond milk.

VEGAN MARGARINE

Look for brands that are not hydrogenated and are trans-fat-free. When baking, opt for vegan margarine sticks, as they tend to have less water content and are easier to measure. One great brand to try is Earth Balance (*www.earthbalancenatural.com*).

NONHYDROGENATED VEGAN SHORTENING

While it does not impart any flavor, shortening is great for making pie crust because it is better able to coat flour than margarine—a key to flaky pastry. For frosting it is also great as it doesn't melt at room temperature. I like the Spectrum brand shortening (*www.spectrumorganics.com*).

VEGETABLE OIL

Here's the rundown on the different oils I recommend for your junk food recipes.

* ❀ Extra-virgin olive oil—This is best for sautéing savory items, and it can also be used for baking where oil is called for, but it can impart a strong flavor.
* ❀ Canola or soybean oil—Its neutral flavor is ideal for baking.
* ❀ Virgin coconut oil—This works best in desserts as it has a light coconut flavor and pairs well with chocolate. As with all oils, look for organic varieties. Nutiva is a brand to try (*www.nutiva.com*).

SUGAR

Table sugar, powdered sugar, and most brown sugar is *not* vegan because of the use of animal bone char to filter it. Most brown sugar starts as white sugar that has molasses added to it later, and powdered sugar starts as table sugar that is then ground into a powder with cornstarch. Alternatives to these sugars are many and include unrefined cane sugar, evaporated cane juice, beet sugar, date sugar, raw or turbinado sugar, and coconut sugar. Here are some one-to-one replacements:

❉ Table sugar—Use vegan cane sugar, beet sugar, or granulated and dehydrated cane juice. Florida Crystals offers a vegan version: *www.floridacrystals.com*.

❉ Brown sugar—Use Sucanat, a whole cane sugar.

❉ Powdered sugar—Use powdered sugar that is made from organic sugar cane. One brand to try is Wholesome Sweeteners: *www.wholesomesweeteners.com*.

❉ Liquid sugars—Use in recipes where you don't mind the additional flavor and softened texture liquid sugars lend to baked goods. Barley malt syrup, brown rice syrup, molasses, corn syrup (not to fear: Although this is a sugar, it's not the same as high-fructose corn syrup), and pure maple syrup are good for baking and candy making. Raw agave syrup is a good replacement for honey. Organic Nectars makes a great agave syrup: *www.organicnectars.com/products.html*.

MEAT ALTERNATIVES

Fake meat is a big part of vegan junk food, so here's a rundown.

❉ Textured vegetable protein (TVP)—Available in bulk bins at health food stores or in packages, TVP is a granular or chunk soy product that is cooked under high pressure and dried. Reconstituted it is an excellent meat replacer where ground meat or small meat chunks are called for. TVP takes on the flavor of whatever it's reconstituted in.

❉ Seitan, or wheat meat—Made from vital wheat gluten and flavorings, seitan has a chewy texture and can be flavored with seasonings to imitate many meat forms. Packaged in broth, prepared seitan is great for stir-fries and many other dishes that call for slabs of meat.

❉ Frozen meat crumbles and patties—The freezer section of your favorite organic grocery should be well stocked with all sorts of brands, including Gardein and Boca.

❉ Hot Dogs—Try Yves Veggie (*www.yvesveggie.com*). For beer brats, try Tofurky brand (*www.tofurky.com*).

❉ Soy chorizo—Made from TVP and spices, this is a vegan version of a Mexican sausage made with marinated and minced meat. Perfect with tofu scramble and tucked into tortillas. Look for "Soyrizo," as it's commonly marketed that way.

❉ Bacon bits—Made from soy and flavorings, these are great on salad or in salad dressing and for imparting bacon flavor and crunch into dips. Frontier's Bac'Uns is a good one to try (*www.frontiercoop.com*).

EGG REPLACER

In baking, flaxseeds do a nice job of replacing eggs. Ground into a powder and then mixed with water, flax-seeds create a gelatinous mixture that replaces the water weight, texture, and some of the fat in eggs, giving you fluffy cakes and cookies. Applesauce is another egg stand-in for baking but can impart an apple flavor and a lot of sweetness (be sure to reduce sugar in recipes if you are using applesauce in place of eggs). Blended tofu is a great binder in vegan quiches and crepes where an egg would add denseness and form. And a teaspoon of nutritional yeast or black salt is great at imparting egg flavor to tofu scrambles or vegan "egg" salad.

CHOCOLATE

Use varieties that do not contain milk and lecithin, an emulsifier that can be made from animals (soy lecithin is vegan).

* Chocolate chips—Look for brands that use evaporated cane juice. This is a brand I like: SunSpire (*www.sunspire.com*).
* Chocolate bars—For specialty candies, bars, and holiday treats, Sjaak's (*www.sjaaks.com*) or Nicobella (*www.nicobellaorganics.com*) offer a wide variety of tasty vegan products.
* Cocoa powder—Cocoa powder is made from cocoa beans and is vegan.
* White bars—Organic Nectars (*www.organicnectars.com*) offers raw organic white chocolate bars.
* White chips—Oppenheimer White Chocolate Chips melt nicely and hold up in a cookie. You can find them online at Food Fight Grocery (*www.foodfightgrocery.com*).

MARSHMALLOWS

Seek out varieties that do not contain gelatin, which is an animal product.

Brands to look for include Sweet & Sara (*www.sweetandsara.com*) and Dandies (*www.chicagosoydairy.com*). For marshmallow fluff, try Suzanne's Ricemellow Crème (*www.suzannes-specialties.com*).

SEASONINGS

Butler Chick-Style Seasoning, Bragg Liquid Aminos, and kelp can help make things taste meaty and/or salty.

CHEESE

An absolute must for pizza or making your savory junk food, there are lots of varieties of cheese shreds on the market. Daiya is one of the more widespread brands: *www.daiyafoods.com*. You can also try nutritional yeast to impart a cheesy flavor in many of your dishes. (It's also high in protein and B12—a vitamin that vegans need to make sure they get enough of in their diets.) A few brands to try include Bob's Red Mill (*www.bobsredmill.com*) and Red Star (*www.redstaryeast.com*).

CHAPTER 1

Breakfast of Champions

Something Savory, Lots of Sweets

Scrambled Tofu Biscuit Sandwich with Sausage Gravy

SERVES 4

- 4 Drop Biscuits (see "Crusts and Carbs"), baked, or 4 English muffins, toasted
- 1 16-ounce carton of firm tofu, drained and broken up into small chunks
- 1 teaspoon oil
- 1 tablespoon nutritional yeast
- ½ teaspoon onion powder
- ⅛ teaspoon turmeric
- 2 teaspoons soy sauce

Pair seasoned scrambled tofu with a savory sauce on a warm toasted biscuit for a sandwich that puts diner fare to shame. Just because it's vegan sausage doesn't mean it lacks the salty, rich flavor of the original. And the creaminess of the gravy can be achieved with nary a cow product in sight.

1. In a medium sauté pan over medium-high heat, cook tofu in 1 teaspoon of oil. Cook for 5 minutes.
2. Stir in nutritional yeast, onion powder, turmeric, and soy sauce, and cook for 2 more minutes. Remove from pan.

Sausage Gravy

- 1 14-ounce package Gimme Lean Sausage
- 1 tablespoon oil
- ¼ cup flour
- 2 cups nondairy milk
- 1 teaspoon salt
- 1 teaspoon pepper

1. In the same pan, cook sausage in oil until browned. Stir in flour and cook for 1 minute. Whisk in the milk. Cook, stirring constantly, until thick and bubbly. Season with salt and pepper.
2. On a biscuit bottom half, spoon ¼ of the scrambled tofu, smother in gravy, cover with the biscuit top, and go to town.

Red Pepper, Caramelized Onion, and Hash Brown Quiche

This eggless quiche gets its sweetness from the peppers and onions, but is otherwise ideal if you're looking for a savory way to start the day. Of course, you could make the crust by slicing and parboiling potatoes, but why bother? Junk food by definition should be easy, and packaged hash browns crisp up just right.

1. Preheat oven to 350°F. Lightly grease a 9" × 13" baking dish or two 8-inch round baking pans.
2. In a medium sauté pan over medium-high heat, sauté onions, peppers, and salt in the oil until onion begins to turn deep golden brown, about 12 minutes. Remove from heat.
3. Press hash browns into prepared baking dish. Cover with onions and peppers.
4. Crumble tofu into a food processor with sour cream, nutritional yeast, garlic powder, salt, and pepper until very smooth.
5. Pour over onions and peppers.
6. Bake for 45-50 minutes, checking periodically to make sure it doesn't brown too soon. If that happens, cover with foil.
7. Allow to cool slightly and dig in.

SERVES 6

1 onion, chopped
1 red pepper, seeded and sliced
3 teaspoons oil
½ teaspoon salt
1 30-ounce package of hash browns
1 16-ounce container firm tofu, drained
¼ cup Vegan Sour Cream (see "Dips for All Seasons")
3 tablespoons nutritional yeast
½ teaspoon garlic powder
1 teaspoon salt
½ teaspoon pepper
¼ teaspoon red pepper flakes

Potato Soyrizo Omelet

SERVES 4

½ cup firm tofu

1½ cups nondairy milk

2 teaspoons oil

1 cup flour

2 tablespoons nutritional yeast

1½ teaspoons baking powder

1 teaspoon salt

1/8 teaspoon turmeric

1 tablespoon chopped chives

2 tablespoons oil

4 potatoes, peeled and diced

6 ounces Soyrizo, vegan Mexican sausage

½ teaspoon pepper

½ teaspoon salt

Nutritional yeast is a vegan's best friend. Add it to tofu and the result is a flavor reminiscent of eggs. Here you get an omelet that's more like a delicate crepe, with bold flavored topping that's anything but delicate.

1. In a blender, blend tofu, milk, and oil until smooth.
2. In a medium bowl, combine flour, nutritional yeast, baking powder, salt, turmeric, and chives. Add the blended ingredients to the flour mixture and mix until very smooth.
3. In a 12-inch skillet, cook ⅓ cup of batter at a time in about 1 teaspoon of oil. Swirl the batter in the pan so that it fills the entire bottom of the pan. Flip the pancake over when the edges look dry and the bottom is golden brown; cook the second side until golden as well. Keep omelets warm covered in foil in the oven at low heat.
4. **To make potato-Soyrizo filling**, heat oil in a large nonstick pan over medium-high heat, add potatoes, and cover with a tight-fitting lid.
5. Cook the potatoes, turning as the bottom ones become golden, removing lid after 15 minutes, and cooking for an additional 5-10 minutes.
6. When the potatoes are golden and cooked through, add the Soyrizo, salt, and pepper to the pan and cook just long enough to heat through.
7. To assemble, place an omelet on a plate and place about ¾ cup of the potato mixture on one half and fold over.

Green Chili and Cheese Omelet

This crepelike omelet serves up medium heat with the addition of green chilies right into the batter. If you like it really hot, opt for jalapeños! Either way, serve it with a generous side of homemade sour cream for dipping.

1. In a blender, blend tofu, soymilk, and oil until smooth.
2. In a medium bowl, combine flour, baking powder, salt, turmeric, and chives. Add the blended ingredients to the flour mixture and mix until very smooth. Stir in the green chilies and cheese.
3. In a 12-inch skillet, cook ⅓ cup of batter at a time in about 1 teaspoon of oil. Swirl the batter in the pan so that it fills the entire bottom of the pan. Flip the pancake over when the edges look dry and the bottom is golden brown; cook the second side until golden as well. Fold into quarters and keep warm as the remainder cooks.
4. Serve with salsa or hot sauce and Vegan Sour Cream.

SERVES 4

½ cup firm tofu
1½ cups soymilk
2 teaspoons oil
1 cup flour
1½ teaspoons baking powder
1 teaspoon salt
1/8 teaspoon turmeric
1 tablespoon chopped chives
1 4-ounce can chopped green chilies
½ cup vegan Cheddar shreds
Optional: salsa or hot sauce and 1 recipe Vegan Sour Cream (see "Dips for All Seasons")

Eggplant Bacon

SERVES 6

2 medium eggplants
½ cup light soy sauce
¼ cup brown sugar
¼ cup apple cider vinegar
¼ cup olive oil
½ teaspoon pepper
⅛ teaspoon liquid smoke
1 teaspoon Cajun-style seasoned salt (optional)

This is so delicious, I've known people (not naming names) who devour a plate in one sitting. Better be preemptive and make two batches! Liquid smoke is the key ingredient here, giving you a smoky bacon flavor without animal by-products.

1. Remove stem end of eggplant, stand eggplant on cut end, and slice down in very thin strips about ⅛-inch thick. A mandolin works great for this.
2. In a large bowl, whisk together soy sauce, brown sugar, vinegar, oil, pepper, liquid smoke, and seasoned salt.
3. Place the eggplant strips in marinade, making sure that each strip gets coated. Allow to marinate in the refrigerator for 3-4 hours, occasionally turning eggplant to be sure all strips are getting evenly marinated.
4. Preheat oven to 350°F. Line a cookie sheet with parchment paper, lightly greased.
5. Place eggplant strips on prepared cookie sheet. Do not overlap, but close together is fine.
6. Bake for about 20 minutes; do not overbake. Eggplant strips will crisp as they cool.
7. Alternatively these can be made in a food dehydrator on medium heat for 24 hours, or when they reach the desired crispness.

Perfect Hash Browns

Move over, Denny's—these hash browns taste even better. They're crispy, salty, and easy to scarf down, but not deep-fried and can be enjoyed in the comfort of your own home.

1. In a 4-quart saucepan over high heat, pour in enough water to cover potatoes; add 1 teaspoon salt. When potatoes boil, cook for 5 minutes, then remove from heat.
2. Grate potatoes into a bowl using a box grater. Gently stir in grated onion and sprinkle on remaining salt and pepper; mix gently.
3. In a large sauté pan over medium-high heat, heat 1 tablespoon of margarine with 1 tablespoon of oil. When the margarine is sizzling, add a heaping tablespoonful of potatoes and flatten slightly with a spatula.
4. Fry two or three spoonfuls at a time, depending on the size of pan. Cook for 5 minutes or until crispy and golden brown, flip over with a spatula, and cook the other side until crispy. Add more oil and margarine to the pan before cooking the next batch.

SERVES 4

- 2 pounds potatoes, peeled and quartered
- 2 teaspoons salt, divided
- ½ teaspoon pepper
- ¼ cup grated onion
- 2 tablespoons vegan margarine
- 2 tablespoons oil

Tater Tot Breakfast Casserole

SERVES 6

- 1 14-ounce package Gimme Lean Sausage
- 1 tablespoon oil
- 1 16-ounce container firm tofu, drained
- ½ cup nutritional yeast
- 2 teaspoons chives, finely chopped
- 2 teaspoons salt
- ½ teaspoon pepper
- ½ teaspoon garlic powder
- 1 16-ounce package frozen Tater Tots

Sometimes I think the fact that Tater Tots exist—and are vegan—proves there is a god. But honestly, when you combine them with the sausage-tofu mixture to make this savory casserole, it borders on divine. This is also a great option for brunch: Prep the night before and bake in the morning. Easy *and* tasty!

1. Preheat oven to 350°F. Lightly oil a 9" × 13" baking dish.
2. In a medium sauté pan over medium-high heat, cook sausage in oil, breaking it up into bite-sized pieces. Cook until browned.
3. In a blender, mix the tofu until very smooth. Add nutritional yeast, chives, salt, pepper, and garlic powder, blending until incorporated.
4. Pour blended mixture into prepared baking dish. Add sausage and mix just to distribute sausage evenly.
5. Arrange Tater Tots on top of tofu mixture.
6. Bake for 45-50 minutes or until potatoes are lightly browned. Tofu will continue to firm as it cools, about 30 minutes.
7. If you're in a decadent mood, serve alongside mimosas and thick slices of toast drenched in vegan margarine.

Sausage in a Blanket with Glazed Apples

Salty-sweet goodness! This recipe combines the best of breakfast foods: the "meaty" flavor of sausage, the fluffy carb-load of pancakes, and the caramel sweetness of homemade applesauce—all rolled into one delicious dish.

1. In a nonstick pan over medium-high heat, cook vegan Breakfast Links until they are heated through and browned. Set aside.
2. In a medium saucepan over medium-high heat, bring water and sugar to a boil, continue to cook for 1 minute, add apples, and cook until sauce has thickened and apples are tender.
3. In a medium bowl, combine flour, oatmeal, baking powder, and salt. Gently stir in milk, sugar, and oil just until combined; a few lumps are okay.
4. Cook each ⅓ cup of pancake batter on a lightly oiled nonstick pan, flipping when bubbles appear on the surface of the pancake; cook the second side until golden.
5. To assemble, roll a Breakfast Link inside each pancake and top with caramelized apples. If you like, add a dollop of Vegan Sour Cream.

SERVES 4

- 1 8-ounce package of Tofurky Breakfast Links (vegan)
- ¼ cup water
- ½ cup brown sugar
- 2 Granny Smith apples, peeled, cored, and chopped
- 1 cup flour
- ¼ cup quick-cooking oatmeal
- 2 teaspoons baking powder
- ½ teaspoon salt
- 1½ cups nondairy milk
- 2 tablespoons sugar
- 1 tablespoon oil
- Optional: 1 recipe Vegan Sour Cream (see "Dips for All Seasons")

Brunch Benedict

SERVES 4

- 1 cup cashews
- 1 cup silken tofu, drained
- 1 tablespoon oil
- ¼ cup lemon juice
- 1 tablespoon nutritional yeast
- ½ teaspoon salt
- ½ teaspoon pepper
- ⅛ teaspoon turmeric
- 1 tablespoon fresh chives, chopped
- 1 package vegan deli slices, such as Tofurky Hickory Smoked
- 4 bagels
- 2 tablespoons margarine

Veganizing this classic brunch dish merely involves perfecting the hollandaise. Cashews provide richness and creaminess, while the lemon and nutritional yeast lend the tang. Problem solved.

1. In a food processor with a fitted blade, process cashews until very fine.
2. Add tofu, oil, lemon juice, nutritional yeast, salt, pepper, and turmeric, and process until very smooth, about 4 minutes.
3. In a medium saucepan on low heat, warm sauce, being very careful not to boil. Remove from heat and stir in chives.
4. While the sauce is heating, toast bagels and spread on margarine. Top each bagel half with four ham slices. Serve topped with warmed hollandaise.

Blueberry Streusel Muffins

Sugar, "butter," shortening, salt, more sugar . . . this is a textbook junk food breakfast, which means it's mouthwatering good. It's also loaded with streusel topping and blueberries. (At least the blueberries have some redeeming qualities.)

1. Preheat oven to 375°F. Line a 12-cup muffin tin with 12 paper liners.
2. In a small bowl, mix flaxseeds, milk, and vinegar; set aside.
3. In a stand mixer or by hand, beat shortening, margarine, sugar, and vanilla until light and fluffy.
4. In a medium bowl, sift flour, baking powder, and salt.
5. Add milk mixture to the shortening and beat until combined. Stir in flour mixture and mix just until combined, fold in blueberries; do not overmix.
6. Fill prepared muffin tins ¾ full.
7. In a medium bowl, combine margarine, brown sugar, sugar, flour, cinnamon, and salt with a fork until margarine is well mixed in and crumbly. Spoon by the heaping tablespoonful onto muffins.
8. Bake for 30 minutes. Cool slightly and slather with vegan margarine so that it melts onto the muffin.

MAKES 12 MUFFINS

- 1 tablespoon flaxseeds
- 1½ cups soymilk
- 1 tablespoon apple cider vinegar
- ½ cup vegetable nonhydrogenated shortening
- 2 tablespoons vegan margarine
- 1¼ cups sugar
- 1 teaspoon vanilla
- 3 cups flour
- 2½ teaspoons baking powder
- ½ teaspoon salt
- 1½ cups fresh blueberries

Streusel Topping

- ½ cup vegan margarine, softened
- ¼ cup brown sugar
- ¼ cup sugar
- $2/3$ cup flour
- ¼ teaspoon cinnamon
- $1/8$ teaspoon salt

Banana Chocolate Chip Muffins

2 tablespoons ground flaxseeds

¾ cup soymilk

1 tablespoon apple cider vinegar

3 cups flour

2 teaspoons baking powder

1 teaspoon baking soda

1 teaspoon salt

1½ cups banana, mashed

1 cup vegetable oil

1½ teaspoons vanilla

1 cup vegan chocolate chips

Streusel

1 cup quick-cooking oats

½ cup sugar

5 tablespoons vegan margarine, softened

½ teaspoon salt

Perfect for when you really want cake for breakfast, these moist muffins emit the most sinful banana-vanilla aroma while they're cooking. The chocolate chips and toasty oatmeal crumble are just icing on the cake—er, muffin.

1. Preheat oven to 375°F. Line a 12-cup muffin tin with 12 paper liners.
2. In a large bowl, mix flaxseeds, milk, and vinegar, and set aside.
3. In a medium bowl, sift flour, baking powder, baking soda, and salt.
4. Add banana, oil, and vanilla to milk mixture, stirring to combine.
5. Stir in flour mixture and mix gently to combine; do not overmix. Fold in chocolate chips.
6. Fill prepared muffin tins ¾ full.
7. In a small bowl, combine oats, sugar, margarine, and salt until crumbly.
8. Spoon on top of muffin batter by the heaping tablespoonful. Press lightly to make sure it doesn't crumble off as the muffin puffs.
9. Bake for 30 minutes or until golden brown.

Pecan Pie Muffins

Who says you can't have pie for breakfast? This just makes it easier because the muffins are quick to prepare and you portion them out into paper-lined tins for individual servings. Although, they're so buttery and nutty, it's unlikely they'll be around for long. . . .

1. Preheat oven to 350°F. Combine milk with flaxseeds and set aside.
2. In a large mixing bowl, combine pecans, sugar, and flour. Add in flaxseed mixture along with the margarine and mix just until combined.
3. Pour into 12 paper-lined muffin tins; fill about ¾ full.
4. Bake for 25 minutes.

MAKES 12 MUFFINS

½ cup nondairy milk
2 tablespoons ground flaxseeds
1 cup crushed pecans
1 cup packed brown sugar
½ cup flour
½ cup vegan margarine, melted

Cheesecake-Filled Crumb Cake

SERVES 6–8

Cake layer

¾ cup soymilk

1 tablespoon apple cider vinegar

2 cups flour

½ teaspoon baking soda

2 teaspoons baking powder

½ teaspoon salt

½ teaspoon cinnamon

½ cup oil

1 cup sugar

Filling

1 8-ounce container vegan cream cheese, softened

⅓ cup sugar

2 tablespoons flour

2 teaspoons lemon zest

½ teaspoon salt

½ teaspoon vanilla extract

Topping

⅔ cup packed brown sugar

½ cup flour

1 teaspoon ground cinnamon

¼ teaspoon nutmeg

½ teaspoon salt

⅔ cup vegan margarine, softened

Another example of a breakfast "dessert" on steroids. For days when crumb cake a la Hostess just won't cut it, go the extra mile and create this creamy sensation.

1. Preheat oven to 350°F. Lightly grease a 9" × 9" baking dish.
2. Combine soymilk and vinegar in a medium bowl; set aside for 5 minutes to thicken.
3. In a large mixing bowl, add flour, baking soda, baking powder, salt, and cinnamon.
4. Add oil and sugar to the soymilk mixture, stirring to combine.
5. Add wet ingredients to the dry and stir until it is completely smooth. Pour half of batter into prepared baking dish.
6. In a medium bowl, mix cream cheese and sugar together. Add flour, lemon zest, salt, and vanilla extract. Pour over batter layer. Cover with remaining batter.
7. In a small bowl, mix together brown sugar, flour, cinnamon, nutmeg, salt, and margarine. Crumble over cake.
8. Bake for 35-40 minutes or until topping is golden brown. Let cool completely before cutting.

Baked Donut Holes 3-Ways

As far as I know, there are only a handful of bakeries that specialize in vegan donuts—and many don't ship 'em. If you're lucky enough to live in a part of the world that has these magical bakeries, by all means seek them out. For everyone else, here's an easy way to make your own.

1. Preheat oven to 350°F. Combine all ingredients in a bowl until smooth.
2. Lightly grease a minimuffin tin. Fill each halfway with batter.
3. Bake for 15 minutes or when a toothpick comes out clean.

Cinnamon Sugar

Roll each donut in ½ cup sugar mixed with 1 teaspoon cinnamon while still warm.

Powdered

Roll each donut in 1 cup powdered sugar while still hot, allow to cool, and roll again.

Chocolate Glaze

Remove donuts from pan and allow to cool. In a microwave-safe bowl, heat 1 package vegan chocolate chips with 1 tablespoon coconut oil in increments of 15 seconds, stirring after each until melted. Using two forks, dip each donut, turning to coat evenly and allowing extra chocolate to drip off. Place on a sheet of parchment paper and refrigerate until chocolate is firm. Alternatively, while chocolate is still wet, sprinkle each donut with chopped nuts, coconut, or sprinkles.

MAKES 24 DONUTS

- 1½ cups flour
- ⅓ cup oil
- ½ cup sugar
- ½ cup nondairy milk
- 1 tablespoon ground flaxseeds
- 1½ teaspoons baking powder
- ½ teaspoon salt
- ¼ teaspoon ground nutmeg

Apple Fritters

1 cup cake flour*

1 tablespoon sugar

1 teaspoon baking powder

¼ teaspoon salt

1 tablespoon ground flaxseeds

½ cup nondairy milk

1½ tablespoons vegan margarine, melted

½ teaspoon vanilla extract

1 cup tart baking apples, peeled and chopped (Granny Smith or Honeycrisp)

Oil for frying

Powdered sugar (for dusting)

When you wake up with a hankering for something warm, sweet, and tart, pad to the kitchen in your jammies and slippers and whip up a batch of these golden-fried Apple Fritters. Your pastries will be ready to eat before your coffee's done brewing. (Mission to remain in PJs: accomplished.)

1. Combine flour, sugar, baking powder, and salt in a large bowl.
2. In a medium bowl, combine flaxseeds, milk, margarine, and vanilla. Add wet ingredients to the dry mixture and stir until just combined. Gently stir in apples. Do not overmix.
3. In a large, deep sauté pan over medium high, bring about an inch of oil to 360°F.
4. Carefully drop batter by heaping tablespoonful into oil, frying until golden brown on each side, about 4-5 minutes.
5. Drain on a paper towel. Sprinkle with powdered sugar.

*NOTE: If you do not have cake flour, measure 2 tablespoons of cornstarch into a 1-cup dry measuring cup and add all-purpose flour until it is full, leveling off flour with the back of a knife. Sift together.

Oatmeal Brûlée with Vanilla Cream Sauce

Did someone say brûlée? For breakfast? You betcha. This super creamy oatmeal has a sugar crust and a fresh berry surprise at the bottom. A drizzle of Vanilla Cream Sauce and you've got the makings of gourmet junk food.

1. Preheat oven to broil setting. Lightly grease four large or six small ovenproof ramekins.
2. In a medium saucepan over medium heat, combine oats, soy creamer or soymilk, brown sugar, margarine, and salt. Cook for 3-5 minutes.
3. Place the berries in prepared ramekins, then top with cooked oatmeal. Sprinkle sugar over each, covering the surface completely.
4. Place ramekins under broiler for about 2 minutes. Watch carefully as once the sugar melts, it will go quickly from golden to burnt.
5. Serve hot with Vanilla Cream Sauce on the side.

SERVES 4

- 1 cup oats
- 1½ cups soy creamer or nondairy milk
- 3 tablespoons brown sugar
- 1 tablespoon vegan margarine
- ½ teaspoon salt
- ½ cup fresh raspberries or blackberries
- ¼ cup sugar

Vanilla Cream Sauce

1. In a medium saucepan over medium-high heat, bring soy creamer and cornstarch to a boil, stirring constantly; continue to cook for 1 minute. Remove from heat and stir in vanilla. This sauce can be served hot or can be refrigerated and served cold.

*NOTE: If you don't have soy creamer, you can use 1 cup nondairy milk plus 1 tablespoon cornstarch to achieve the same creamy results.

- 1 cup soy creamer*
- 1 teaspoon cornstarch
- 2 teaspoons vanilla

Pumpkin Pie Pancakes with Cinnamon Syrup

SERVES 4

1 cup nondairy milk

2 tablespoons ground flaxseeds

½ cup canned pure pumpkin

2 tablespoons oil

1¼ cups flour

1 tablespoon sugar

2 teaspoons baking powder

1 teaspoon pumpkin pie spice

½ teaspoon salt

These pancakes are easier than pie—with all the same flavors. Top with a buttery cinnamon syrup that'll make your omnivorous friends jealous.

1. In a medium bowl, combine milk, flaxseeds, pumpkin, and oil, and stir well.
2. In a large bowl, sift together flour, sugar, baking powder, pumpkin pie spice, and salt. Add wet ingredients to the dry mixture, stirring gently until just combined. A few lumps are okay.
3. Cook ⅓ cup of pancake batter on a lightly oiled nonstick pan, flipping when bubbles appear on the surface of the pancake; cook the second side until golden.

½ cup vegan margarine

½ cup brown sugar

1 teaspoon vanilla

2 teaspoons cinnamon

Cinnamon Syrup

1. In a small saucepan over medium-high heat, stir the margarine until bubbly and golden brown. Add the sugar, stirring constantly, and cook until it comes back to a boil. Remove from heat and add vanilla and cinnamon.
2. Serve warm over piping hot pancakes.

Peanut Butter Pancakes with Strawberry Jam

A new twist on a classic lunch treat, this breakfast PB&J satisfies the urge to be back in middle school with your homies. (Don't be fooled by the flaxseeds! I'm not trying to make this healthy—mixed with milk, they're a great substitute binder in place of eggs.)

1. In a small bowl, mix milk and flaxseeds, then set aside.
2. In a medium bowl, whisk together flour, sugar, baking powder, and salt.
3. Mix peanut butter and vanilla into milk mixture. Stir well. Add to flour mixture and stir just until combined. Do not overmix; a few lumps are okay.
4. Cook each ⅓ cup of pancake batter on a lightly oiled nonstick pan, flipping when bubbles appear on the surface of the pancake and then cooking the second side until golden.
5. Serve with a dollop of your favorite strawberry jam.

SERVES 4

- 1 cup nondairy milk
- 2 tablespoons ground flaxseeds
- 1½ cups flour
- 1 tablespoon sugar
- 2 teaspoons baking powder
- ½ teaspoon salt
- ½ cup peanut butter
- ½ teaspoon vanilla
- Strawberry jam

Cinnamon Roll French Toast

SERVES 4

1½ cups nondairy milk

1½ tablespoons flour

2 tablespoons nutritional yeast

2 teaspoons cinnamon

1 tablespoon sugar

½ teaspoon salt

6 slices day-old thick-sliced French bread

Oil for frying

Cinnamon Glaze

3 tablespoons vegan margarine, melted

1 teaspoon cinnamon

2 teaspoons sugar

Icing

1 cup powdered sugar

1 tablespoon vegan margarine, softened

1 teaspoon vanilla

2 tablespoons nondairy milk

Here's the perfect solution for your leftover French bread, and one that rivals the most gooey, sweet, decadent cinnamon rolls found in a tube in the refrigerator aisle. Indulge in this cinnamon spin on traditional French toast when the mood strikes.

1. In a shallow dish, whisk together milk, flour, nutritional yeast, cinnamon, sugar, and salt.
2. **To make the glaze**, in a small bowl, mix together the melted margarine, cinnamon, and sugar until sugar melts. Set aside.
3. Dip bread into milk mixture and fry in a medium sauté pan over medium heat with 1 teaspoon of oil until browned on each side. Remove from pan and spread with a teaspoon of cinnamon-margarine mixture. Repeat for the rest of bread slices.
4. **To make the icing**, in a small bowl, combine sugar, margarine, vanilla, and milk with a whisk until smooth. Drizzle over hot French toast and pair with Eggplant Bacon and fresh-squeezed OJ for a brunch extravaganza.

Sticky Caramel Baked French Toast

A bit more time-intensive, but because this sits before it bakes, the bread soaks up the caramel and the results are super sticky and rich.

1. In a saucepan over medium heat, stir sugar, margarine, and agave syrup until it comes to a boil. Continue to cook for 1 minute and remove from heat.
2. Lightly grease a 9" × 13" baking dish and pour mixture into prepared baking dish. Place bread over caramel.
3. In a small bowl, mix milk, flour, nutritional yeast, cinnamon, vanilla, sugar, and salt. Pour over bread. Let it sit for at least 1 hour or overnight in the refrigerator.
4. When ready to cook, preheat oven to 350°F and bake for 25-30 minutes, until golden brown.

SERVES 6

- 1 cup packed brown sugar
- ½ cup vegan margarine
- 2 tablespoons agave syrup
- 6 slices day-old thick-sliced bread cut in half to make triangles
- 1 cup nondairy soy creamer or nondairy milk
- 1½ tablespoons flour
- 2 tablespoons nutritional yeast
- 1 teaspoon cinnamon
- 1 teaspoon vanilla
- ¼ cup sugar
- ½ teaspoon salt

Eggnog French Toast with Butter Rum Sauce

SERVES 4

6 slices day-old thick-sliced bread
1½ cups nondairy soy eggnog
1½ tablespoons flour
2 tablespoons nutritional yeast
½ teaspoon cinnamon
¼ cup sugar
½ teaspoon salt
Oil for frying

Here's a festive breakfast treat that's perfect to serve to your vegan and omnivore friends and relatives—they'll never know what hit them. The eggnog flavor screams "Holiday!" and the Butter Rum Sauce is all about celebrating.

1. In a shallow dish, whisk together eggnog, flour, nutritional yeast, cinnamon, sugar, and salt until combined.
2. Dip each piece of bread into eggnog mixture. Fry in a large sauté pan over medium-high heat with 1 teaspoon of oil until browned on each side.

Butter Rum Sauce

1 cup sugar
½ cup vegan margarine
½ cup nondairy soy creamer or nondairy milk
1/8 teaspoon rum extract or 2 tablespoons rum

1. In a small saucepan over medium heat, combine sugar, margarine, and milk, stirring constantly. Bring to a boil and continue to cook for 1 minute. Remove from heat.
2. Stir in rum extract and serve over French toast.

Waffles with Creamy Maple Sauce

If you don't currently own a waffle iron, you might want to knock on your neighbor's door and borrow one ASAP because it would be a shame if you couldn't make these crisp, nutty-flax waffles and top them with a creamy, sweet maple sauce reminiscent of a donut glaze. Uh, what are you waiting for?

1. In a small bowl, mix milk with flaxseeds and set aside.
2. In a large bowl, combine flour, baking powder, salt, and sugar.
3. Stir the oil into the milk mixture. Add wet ingredients to the large bowl and mix thoroughly.
4. Cook according to the manufacturer's directions for your waffle maker.

SERVES 4

1 cup nondairy milk
1 tablespoon ground flaxseeds
1 cup flour
2 teaspoons baking powder
¼ teaspoon salt
1 tablespoon sugar
¼ cup oil

Creamy Maple Sauce

1. In a saucepan, combine all the ingredients, stirring until very smooth and bubbling. Add more milk a tablespoon at a time. If it becomes too thick, serve immediately on waffles.

2 cups powdered sugar
1 tablespoon maple syrup
¼ cup of nondairy soy creamer or nondairy milk

Lemon Poppy Seed Waffles with Lemon Curd

SERVES 4

¾ cup nondairy milk

¼ cup lemon juice

1 tablespoon ground flaxseed

Zest of one lemon

1 tablespoon sugar

¼ cup oil

1 cup flour

2 teaspoons baking powder

2 teaspoons poppy seeds

¼ teaspoon salt

These could just as easily fit into the dessert chapter, but as the saying goes, life is short, so eat dessert first. In this case, the first meal is breakfast, so it all makes sense. Sweet and tart, the yummy Lemon Curd could be eaten on its own by the spoonful (not that I've ever done that or anything).

1. In a small bowl, mix milk, lemon juice, flaxseed, lemon zest, sugar, and oil, then set aside.
2. In a large bowl, combine flour, baking powder, poppy seeds, and salt.
3. Stir milk mixture into flour mixture and mix thoroughly.
4. Cook according to the manufacturer's directions for your waffle maker.

¼ cup coconut milk

½ cup sugar

3 tablespoons cornstarch

⅛ teaspoon salt

Zest of two lemons

¼ cup lemon juice

Lemon Curd

1. Combine coconut milk or water, sugar, cornstarch, salt, and lemon zest in a saucepan. Heat on medium, stirring constantly until mixture comes to a full boil, then cook for 1 minute.
2. Remove from heat and stir in lemon juice. Serve warm over waffles. Be sure to refrigerate any leftover curd. (That is, if you have any leftovers!)

Strawberry Daiquiri Crepes

There's no need to make a brunch cocktail to go alongside this dish because the rum is already part of the sauce. But these won't make you tipsy; the prevalent flavor is that of fresh and frozen strawberries alongside delicate crepe quarters.

1. In a large mixing bowl, whisk together flour, milk, club soda, margarine, nutritional yeast, and salt until smooth. Allow mixture to stand on counter for 10 minutes.
2. Heat a crepe pan or a shallow skillet over medium-high heat. Add about a teaspoon oil and swirl to coat bottom of pan. Add about ¼ cup of crepe mixture to pan and swirl again to coat entire bottom of pan with batter. Flip when edges look dry and bottom is just golden.
3. Transfer to a plate, fold each crepe into quarters, and cover with a towel to keep warm.

SERVES 4

- 1 cup flour
- ½ cup nondairy milk
- ½ cup club soda
- ¼ cup vegan margarine, melted
- 1 tablespoon nutritional yeast
- ¼ teaspoon salt
- Oil for pan
- Fresh strawberries hulled and quartered
- Powdered sugar for garnish

Daiquiri Sauce

1. In a small saucepan, heat strawberries and sugar over medium heat. Cook until liquid is reduced by half. Remove from heat, then stir in lime juice and rum.
2. Serve hot poured over folded crepes garnished with fresh strawberries and powdered sugar.

- 4 ounces frozen strawberries
- ½ cup powdered sugar
- $1/8$ cup lime juice
- ¼ cup rum

CHAPTER 2

Deli Favorites

*Sandwiches, Wraps,
Burgers, and Sliders*

Sesame Tempeh Sandwich

SERVES 4

4 tablespoons light soy sauce

1 tablespoon sesame seeds, toasted

2 tablespoons balsamic vinegar

2 teaspoons ginger, minced

2 teaspoons sesame oil

1 clove garlic, crushed

1 8-ounce package tempeh, sliced into ¼-inch slices

2 tablespoons peanut oil or olive oil

1 cup cabbage, very thinly sliced

½ cup red cabbage, very thinly sliced

1 carrot, cut into long thin strands

2 tablespoons seasoned rice vinegar

2 tablespoons vegan mayonnaise

1 teaspoon light soy sauce

½ teaspoon sesame oil

4 split sandwich buns

Hot Chili sauce or Sriracha

Hoisin sauce

What would you prefer: A typical drive-thru burger or tempeh stewed in an Asian-inspired marinade, then pan-fried and topped with a fresh slaw and hot sauce? No contest, right?

1. In a shallow dish, combine soy sauce, sesame seeds, vinegar, ginger, sesame oil, and garlic. Add tempeh slices, turning to coat pieces. Marinate 1 hour, turning occasionally. Remove from marinade and set aside.
2. In a medium sauté pan over medium-high heat, sauté tempeh in peanut oil until golden on each side, about 4 minutes.
3. In a medium bowl, toss cabbage and carrots with rice vinegar, mayonnaise, soy sauce, and sesame oil.
4. On each split bun, place a few heaping tablespoons of slaw. Divide tempeh between the four rolls and top with an optional drizzle of chili sauce and/or hoisin sauce.

Grilled Portobello Sandwich with Garlicky Horseradish Mayonnaise

Portobello mushrooms have a magical quality that makes them feel and taste like meat, which means they're a good friend of most vegans. This hearty sandwich will satisfy any roast beef-like craving as well as deliver a horseradish zinger.

1. In a small bowl, mix together mayonnaise, horseradish, mustard, and garlic. Set aside.
2. In a shallow dish, combine balsamic, Merlot, Worcestershire sauce, salt, and pepper. Place portobellos in marinade, turning to coat. Let marinate for 20 minutes, turning occasionally.
3. In a large grill pan or sauté pan over medium-high heat, sauté each portobello in olive oil about 3–4 minutes per side until tender. Remove from heat. Slice into ½-inch thick strips.
4. Split and toast French bread rolls, spread a heaping teaspoonful of mayonnaise on each side. Top with spinach, divide mushrooms between the four sandwiches, and enjoy.

SERVES 4

- ½ cup vegan mayonnaise
- 1 tablespoon prepared horseradish
- 1 teaspoon Dijon mustard
- 1 clove garlic, minced
- 2 tablespoons balsamic vinegar
- 1 tablespoon Merlot wine
- 1 tablespoon vegan Worcestershire sauce
- 1 teaspoon salt
- 1 teaspoon pepper
- 4 medium portobello mushrooms
- 3 tablespoons olive oil for cooking
- 4 French bread rolls
- 2 cups baby spinach, washed and dried

Open-Faced Grilled Veggie Sandwich with Creamy Pesto

SERVES 4

- 1 recipe Basil Pesto (See "Dips for All Seasons")
- ½ cup vegan mayonnaise
- 1 red bell pepper, cut into thick planks
- 1 small eggplant, cut into ¼-inch rounds
- 1 red onion, sliced
- 2 tablespoons oil
- 1 tablespoon balsamic vinegar
- 1 teaspoon salt
- ½ teaspoon pepper
- 1 large tomato, sliced thick
- 1 baguette, cut on the diagonal into 1-inch slices
- 2 cloves garlic
- 1 recipe Balsamic Reduction (see "Dips for All Seasons")

A sandwich piled high with veggies doesn't seem to qualify as junk food, but once you smear on creamy pesto and drizzle with sweetly acidic balsamic vinegar, it inches closer. No matter—this is quick to prepare and plain delicious.

1. In a small bowl, combine pesto with mayonnaise. Set aside.
2. Preheat oven to broil, ready your barbecue, or heat a grill pan over medium-high heat.
3. In a large bowl, toss bell pepper, eggplant, and onion with oil, balsamic vinegar, salt, and pepper.
4. Cook bell pepper, eggplant, and onion using preferred method until vegetables are charred on each side and tender. Remove from heat and cook tomato slices, 1 minute on each side.
5. Toast bread slightly just until crisp but not browned. Rub each slice with garlic and spread on a heaping tablespoonful of pesto mayonnaise.
6. Layer peppers, eggplant, onion, and tomato on top of each bread slice.
7. Drizzle with Balsamic Reduction.

Messy Barbecue Sandwich with Tangy Sweet Mustard Red Potatoes

Curb your craving for barbecue with this vegan rendition. I always eat this sandwich with the potatoes, so I can't imagine one without the other. The tang of the mustard in the creamy textured potato salad perfectly complements the sweet and spicy sauce.

1. In a large stockpot, boil enough salted water to cover potatoes, then cook for about 15 minutes or until fork-tender. Drain.
2. In a medium saucepan, combine barbecue sauce and tempeh, and heat to a boil. Turn heat down to medium and let simmer.
3. In a sauté pan over medium-high heat, sauté onions in oil until golden, stirring occasionally, about 10 minutes. Add to barbecue mixture. Remove from heat.
4. In a medium bowl, combine mayonnaise, agave, Dijon mustard, vinegar, salt, and pepper. Toss potatoes in dressing.
5. On each toasted French bread roll, spread on mayonnaise and spoon on barbecue tempeh. Serve with red potatoes.

MAKES 4 SANDWICHES

- 1 teaspoon salt
- 1 pound small red potatoes, cut in half
- 3 cups sweet and tangy barbecue sauce
- 2 8-ounce packages tempeh, crumbled
- 1 tablespoon oil
- 1 onion, diced
- 1 teaspoon salt
- ½ cup vegan mayonnaise plus some to spread on sandwich
- 4 tablespoons raw agave
- 1 tablespoon Dijon mustard
- 1 tablespoon apple cider vinegar
- 1 teaspoon salt
- ½ teaspoon pepper
- 4 French bread sandwich rolls

Portobello Cheesesteak

SERVES 4

- 1 pound portobello mushrooms
- 1 tablespoon oil
- 1 teaspoon vegan Worcestershire sauce
- 1 teaspoon salt
- 1 teaspoon pepper
- 1 tablespoon oil
- 1 green bell pepper, seeded and sliced
- 1 red bell pepper, seeded and sliced
- 1 onion, thinly sliced
- 4 sandwich rolls
- 2 cups vegan mozzarella shreds

A vegan take on the traditional cheesesteak: Meaty to the tooth, the savory sautéed mushrooms mix with peppers and onions in a toasted roll. Top it with loads of cheese for melty goodness.

1. Preheat oven to broil.
2. Slice portobellos into ¼-inch slices. In a large bowl, toss mushrooms with oil, Worcestershire sauce, salt, and pepper. In a medium sauté pan over medium-high heat, sauté mushrooms until tender. Remove from pan.
3. Add another tablespoon of oil to the pan and sauté peppers and onions until onions are golden and peppers are tender. Add mushrooms back to the pan and stir.
4. Spoon mushrooms and peppers into sandwich rolls; place ½ cup cheese on each. Place sandwiches under broiler and cook until cheese is melted and bread is toasted, about 4-5 minutes.

Chickpea Tuna Melt

Cross a garbanzo-bean base with some sea kelp, lemon juice, crunchy celery, and onion for the most mouthwatering mock tuna sandwich this side of the Atlantic. Serve the slightly briny sandwich open-faced on a fresh ciabatta roll to complete the mock experience.

1. Preheat oven to broil.
2. In a large bowl, lightly mash garbanzo beans to a coarse texture. Mix in celery, onion, mayonnaise, lemon, kelp granules, salt, and lemon pepper. Stir to combine completely.
3. Split ciabatta rolls and brush each cut side lightly with olive oil. Divide the Chickpea Tuna between the four halves and top with ½ cup cheese.
4. Broil until cheese is melted and bread is toasted, 4-5 minutes.

*NOTE: If you cannot find kelp granules, you can substitute a 2" × 2" piece of nori or sushi roll sheets, chop it very fine with a knife, or run it through a coffee grinder to get a very fine chop.

SERVES 4

- 1 15-ounce can garbanzo beans, drained and rinsed
- 1 cup celery, chopped
- ½ cup red onion, chopped
- 1 cup vegan mayonnaise
- 1 tablespoon fresh-squeezed lemon juice
- 1 teaspoon kelp granules*
- 1 teaspoon salt
- ½ teaspoon lemon pepper
- 2 ciabatta rolls
- Olive oil
- 1 cup vegan mozzarella shreds

Eggplant BLTA with Garlic Chive Mayo

SERVES 4

1 cup vegan mayonnaise

1 clove garlic, pressed

2 tablespoons chives, minced

1 teaspoon salt

½ teaspoon pepper

8 slices sourdough bread

1 recipe Eggplant Bacon
(see "Breakfast of
Champions")
or

1 5-ounce package of LightLife
Smart Bacon, cooked

1 medium tomato, sliced

6–8 leaves butter leaf lettuce

1 ripe avocado, sliced
Salt and pepper

When you think of comfort food, it doesn't get much better than the BLT. Make this one with Eggplant Bacon, avocado, and garlicky mayo for a vegan version that raises the bar on the original.

1. In a small bowl, combine mayonnaise with garlic (garlic should go through a garlic press or mash with the side of a heavy knife), chives, salt, and pepper.
2. Toast the sourdough bread until golden and place about ½ tablespoon of garlic mayonnaise on each slice.
3. Pile on Eggplant Bacon, tomato, lettuce, avocado, and salt and pepper to taste.

Bacon Egg Salad

Vegan bacon bits give a salty tang to this salad, which features tofu and garbanzo beans masquerading as eggs. French bread croutons add the crunch required in any self-respecting junk food.

1. Preheat oven to 350°F. Line a baking sheet with parchment paper.
2. In a medium bowl, toss French bread with olive oil. Place on prepared baking sheet. Bake croutons until golden brown and crunchy, about 8 minutes, tossing halfway through to toast evenly. Remove from oven.
3. In a large bowl, slightly mash garbanzo beans. Mix in tofu.
4. In a small bowl, stir together relish, Dijon mustard, bacon bits, salt, and pepper. Add to the tofu mixture with croutons and stir to combine.
5. Serve large scoops on butter leaf lettuce or on a plate if the lettuce feels too healthy.

SERVES 3–4

- 2 cups French bread, cut into 2-inch cubes
- 2 tablespoons olive oil
- 1 15-ounce can garbanzo beans, drained and rinsed
- 4 ounces firm tofu, drained and chopped into ¼-inch dice
- 2 tablespoons pickle relish
- ¾ cup vegan mayonnaise
- 1 tablespoon Dijon mustard
- 1 tablespoon vegan bacon bits
- 1 teaspoon salt
- ½ teaspoon pepper
- 6–8 leaves butter leaf lettuce (optional)

Meatball Subwich

- 2 cups vegetable broth
- ¾ cup textured vegetable protein
- 2 tablespoons ground flaxseeds
- ¼ cup water
- ½ cup cooked brown rice
- ½ cup onion, chopped
- 1 teaspoon oil
- 1 clove garlic, chopped
- 1 tablespoon tomato paste
- 1 teaspoon vegan Worcestershire sauce
- 1 teaspoon light soy sauce
- ½ cup bread crumbs
- ½ cup walnuts, finely minced
- ½ teaspoon dried oregano
- ½ teaspoon dried parsley
- ½ teaspoon dried basil
- 4 French bread rolls
- 2 cups marinara sauce
- 1 cup vegan mozzarella shreds

If you're in a rush, you can use store-bought vegan meatballs, but it's simple enough to make them from scratch and they taste *way* better. Onion, garlic, walnuts, and herbs are the stars of these brown rice TVP-based meatballs. Wedge them into a slab of French bread, smother in marinara, and top with a minimountain of cheese for lunch nirvana.

1. Preheat oven to 350°F. Line a baking sheet with parchment paper.
2. In a small saucepan, bring vegetable broth to a boil and add textured vegetable protein. Turn heat off and allow TVP to reconstitute for 10 minutes. Drain very well, squeezing liquid out.
3. In a small bowl, mix flaxseeds with ¼ cup water and set aside.
4. In a medium sauté pan, cook onions in 1 teaspoon oil, stirring until translucent. Add garlic and sauté 1 more minute. Remove from heat.
5. In a large bowl, combine all the ingredients and mix with hands until very well combined. If the mixture is too dry to be shaped into a ball, add 1 more tablespoon of tomato paste. If mixture is too wet, add ¼ cup bread crumbs at a time until you can easily shape into 1½-inch balls.
6. Place balls on prepared baking sheet.
7. Bake for 25-30 minutes, carefully turning meatballs halfway through cooking. Meatballs are done when they turn a deep golden brown. Set oven to broil.
8. Open French bread roll without separating two halves, place four or five meatballs in each roll, spoon on ½ cup marinara, and top each with ¼ cup cheese.
9. Place sandwiches under broiler until cheese is melted and bread is toasted, about 5 minutes.

Chicken Salad with Walnuts, Apples, and Celery

To cook nonvegan versions of classic junk food, you need to become familiar with such ingredients as vegan chicken bouillon and TVP (textured vegetable protein), both of which are featured here. The bouillon imparts a "chickeny" flavor sans actual chicken, and TVP has a texture that mimics the mouth-feel of the meat. Try Bob's Red Mill—they make a mean TVP.

1. Place TVP in a medium heatproof bowl. Heat vegetable broth and chicken bouillon base to a vigorous boil. Pour over TVP and let sit for 10 minutes. Drain, reserving liquid. When cool enough to touch, place TVP in a kitchen towel and squeeze out excess liquid.
2. In a medium bowl, combine mayonnaise, salt, pepper, Dijon mustard, celery, red onion, walnuts, and apple. Stir in TVP.
3. Serve on split ciabatta rolls with lettuce and extra mayonnaise.

SERVES 4

½ cup small-grain textured vegetable protein

2 cups vegetable broth

1 teaspoon vegan chicken bouillon base

1 cup vegan mayonnaise, plus some for spreading on bread

1 teaspoon salt

½ teaspoon pepper

2 teaspoons vegan Dijon mustard

½ cup celery, finely chopped

¼ cup red onion, finely chopped

¼ cup walnuts, chopped

1 apple, cored and chopped

4 ciabatta sandwich rolls

Green leaf lettuce

Pad Thai Wrap

SERVES 4

1 8-ounce package flat rice noodles

1 teaspoon oil

1 6-ounce package savory baked tofu, teriyaki flavor

¼ cup soy sauce

3 tablespoons lemon juice

1 tablespoon brown sugar

1 teaspoon chili paste

2 tablespoons peanut oil

1 onion, thinly sliced

2 cloves garlic, chopped

1 red chili, sliced

3 green onions, green and white parts, cut thinly on the diagonal

¼ cup peanuts, chopped

¼ cup cilantro, finely chopped

6 tortillas or flatbread

3 cups mesclun greens

1 recipe Spicy Peanut Sauce (see "Dips for All Seasons")

When Asian food is all you crave, you'll want to whip up these savory-sweet wraps. They include the five essential junk food groups: carbs (noodles), meat (teriyaki tofu), sugar, spice (red chili), and peanuts. *Sayonara*, takeout!

1. In a large saucepan, boil enough water to cook noodles, about 10 minutes or until tender. Drain. Toss in 1 teaspoon oil to prevent noodles from sticking together.
2. Slice tofu into thin strips.
3. In a small bowl, combine soy sauce, lemon juice, brown sugar, and chili paste. Set aside.
4. In a large sauté pan over high heat, coat pan with peanut oil and sauté onion, garlic, and red chili until onions are translucent. Add noodles, tofu, and green onion. Toss with tongs to mix well. Add the soy sauce mixture. Stir well. Remove from heat. Stir in peanuts and cilantro.
5. On each tortilla or flatbread, place about ½ cup Pad Thai, ½ cup mesclun greens, and drizzle on Spicy Peanut Sauce. Wrap into a cylinder, secure with a toothpick in two places, and cut in half.

Barbecued Tempeh Wrap

This sandwich is a favorite with my catering clients—who range from students to rock stars, so that's saying a lot! This takes no more than 10 minutes to assemble, so it's perfect for when you need to eat fast. Resist leaving out any of the ingredients. They work in harmony, creating a most mouthwatering wrap.

1. In a medium bowl, mix barbecue sauce and tempeh crumble.
2. For each wrap, spread on a tablespoon of mayonnaise, ¼ of the barbecue tempeh, ½ cup mesclun greens, ¼ of the apple slices, ¼ of the onion slices, and a sprinkle of cilantro.
3. Drizzle on Creamy Ranch Dressing.
4. Wrap and devour!

SERVES 4

1 cup barbecue sauce

1 8-ounce package tempeh, crumbled

4 whole-wheat tortillas or lavash flatbread

4 tablespoons vegan mayonnaise

2 cups mesclun greens

1 green apple, cored and sliced thin

½ red onion, sliced thin

¼ cup fresh cilantro

1 recipe Creamy Ranch Dressing (see "Dips for All Seasons")

Caesar Salad Tofu Wrap with Barbecue Potato Chips

SERVES 4

1 head romaine, washed, dried, torn into bite-sized pieces

¾ cup Caesar Salad Dressing (see "Dips for All Seasons")

4 whole-wheat tortillas or lavash flatbread

2 6-ounce packages savory baked tofu, cut into strips

1 medium tomato, sliced

½ red onion, sliced thinly

Drench this wrap with the creamy delicious dressing and devour. (Leave out tomatoes and onions if you want to up the junk food factor.) The nuked Barbecue Potato Chips get super crispy and are a must on the side!

1. In a large bowl, toss lettuce with about ½ cup of dressing.
2. On each tortilla, spread a few teaspoons of Caesar Salad Dressing and add a large handful of lettuce, then top with tofu, tomatoes, and onions.
3. Wrap tightly and cut in half.

SERVES 4

1–2 potatoes, peeled, sliced paper-thin

1 tablespoon olive oil

½ teaspoon paprika

½ teaspoon salt

½ teaspoon sugar

¼ teaspoon garlic powder

¼ teaspoon onion powder

¼ teaspoon chili powder

Barbecue Potato Chips

1. In a medium bowl, toss potatoes, olive oil, paprika, salt, sugar, garlic powder, onion powder, and chili powder until evenly coated.
2. Line microwave-safe plate with parchment paper. In small batches, arrange potatoes in a single layer.
3. Microwave uncovered for 3-5 minutes, turning with tongs halfway through (cooking time will depend on your microwave). Look for even browning.
4. Remove from microwave; chips will crisp as they cool.

Tofu Lettuce Wrap with Peanut Sauce

Here's the vegan version of the popular lettuce wraps you find in restaurants. Savory baked tofu is something that's widely available, so experiment with different types to find the flavor and texture you like best.

1. In a large sauté pan over medium-high heat, sauté garlic, ginger, and red chilies in oil for 3 minutes. Add tofu, sesame oil, soy sauce, and hoisin sauce. Cook until sauce comes to a boil. Remove from heat.
2. In a large bowl, combine carrots, cabbage, bean sprouts, green onions, cilantro, and lime juice.
3. On each leaf of butter lettuce, put a heaping tablespoonful of cabbage mixture topped with a heaping tablespoon of tofu mixture. Drizzle with Spicy Peanut Sauce.

SERVES 4

- 1 tablespoon oil
- 2 cloves garlic, chopped
- 1 tablespoon ginger, minced
- 1–2 red chilies, deseeded and sliced
- 1 6-ounce package savory baked tofu, diced
- 1 teaspoon sesame oil
- ½ cup soy sauce
- 1 tablespoon hoisin sauce
- Juice of two limes
- ½ cup shredded carrots
- ½ cup shredded cabbage
- ½ cup bean sprouts
- 3 green onions, cut thinly on the diagonal
- ¼ cup cilantro, finely chopped
- 6–8 whole leaves, butter leaf lettuce
- 1 recipe Spicy Peanut Sauce (see "Dips for All Seasons")

Sloppy Joes

½ cup small-grain textured vegetable protein (such as Bob's Red Mill TVP)

2 cups vegetable broth

1 teaspoon vegan beef bouillon base

1 tablespoon oil

½ onion, chopped

¼ cup finely chopped carrot

1 clove garlic, chopped

1 teaspoon salt

½ teaspoon pepper

2 tablespoons brown sugar

2 teaspoons balsamic vinegar

1 teaspoon vegan Worcestershire sauce

4 tablespoons tomato paste

1 cup tomato sauce

4 hamburger buns

Put this up against the meat version of a sloppy joe in a taste test, and I'd bet most wouldn't be able to tell the difference—they're amazingly similar in flavor and texture.

1. In a medium heatproof bowl, place TVP. Heat vegetable broth and beef bouillon base to a vigorous boil. Pour over TVP and let sit for 10 minutes. Drain, reserving liquid. When cool enough to touch, place TVP in a kitchen towel and squeeze out excess liquid.
2. In a large sauté pan over medium-high heat, sauté onions and carrots in oil until onions are translucent. Add garlic to pan and cook for 1 minute. Add TVP to pan and cook, stirring often, until TVP is browned, about 5 minutes.
3. Add salt, pepper, brown sugar, balsamic vinegar, Worcestershire sauce, tomato paste, and tomato sauce, stirring well. Add ½ cup of reserved broth and bring to a boil. Turn heat down to medium and cook for 10 minutes.

Black Bean Burger with Onion Rings

This burger is made extra "junky" with the addition of those deliciously salty and crunchy canned fried onion strips. You know the ones: They're in the same family as canned potato sticks. In any case, mix 'em in for extra kick. If you have time, pair with homemade beer-battered onion rings for a totally amazing combo.

1. In a large bowl with a potato masher, mash the black beans until they are coarsely chopped but not mushy. Add the bread crumbs, fried onions, mayonnaise, cilantro, salt, pepper, garlic powder, barbecue sauce, ketchup, and chili powder. Mix by hand until all ingredients are combined.
2. Shape by hand into patties. If burgers stick to your hands, add ½ cup bread crumbs; if burgers don't hold together, add 2 tablespoons mayonnaise.
3. On a grill pan or heavy skillet over medium-high heat, cook each burger in a teaspoon of oil about 4-5 minutes on each side. Patties can also be baked on a parchment-lined cookie sheet in a 375°F oven for 25 minutes, turning patties halfway through cooking.
4. Place each patty on a toasted hamburger bun with selected garnishes. Don't forget to top with two onion ring strips!

SERVES 4

- 1 15-ounce can black beans, drained and rinsed
- ¾ cup bread crumbs
- 1 cup canned French's French Fried Onions, crushed
- 2 tablespoons vegan mayonnaise
- 2 tablespoons cilantro, finely chopped
- 1 teaspoon salt
- ½ teaspoon pepper
- ½ teaspoon garlic powder
- 1 tablespoon barbecue sauce
- 1 tablespoon ketchup
- 1 teaspoon chili powder
   Oil for cooking
   Hamburger buns
   Vegan mayonnaise, barbecue sauce, ketchup, and pickles for garnish

Crispy Chicken Ranch Burger

4 SERVINGS

1 cup ice water
1½ cups all-purpose flour
1 teaspoon baking powder
1 teaspoon salt
½ teaspoon pepper
  Canola oil for frying
1 16-ounce package firm tofu, drained and cut through the width of the block, making 4 patties
1 recipe Creamy Ranch Dressing (see "Dips for All Seasons")
1 ripe avocado, sliced
  Lettuce, washed and leafed
1 medium tomato, sliced
½ onion, thinly sliced
4 hamburger buns

Fry up those slices of tofu with a tempura batter and make like a chicken sandwich. Be sure to drench these delicious patties with a generous helping of Creamy Ranch Dressing to complete the deep-fried feast.

1. In a medium bowl, combine the ice water, flour, baking powder, salt, and pepper, stir until just combined; a few lumps are fine.
2. In a deep 2-quart pot, heat on medium-high enough oil to submerge the tofu patties. You'll know the oil is hot enough when bubbles appear around the base of a chopstick inserted into the oil. Dip the tofu patties into the tempura batter, turning to completely coat, and carefully place in the heated oil. Fry about 1-2 minutes, turning when light golden brown, then fry the second side 1-2 minutes longer. Set on paper towels to drain. Repeat for all four patties.
3. Spoon a tablespoon of Creamy Ranch Dressing on buns and add tofu patty. Garnish with avocado, lettuce, onion, tomato, and extra Creamy Ranch Dressing.

Curry Mushroom Burger with Mango Chutney

A taste of India, without needing to find the takeout menu or tip the delivery boy. The classic junk combo of spicy and savory-sweet flavors are on display here: Baked tofu supplies the savory; mango chutney supplies the sweet.

1. In a medium sauté pan over medium-high heat, sauté mushrooms, onion, and garlic in oil until onions are translucent. Add salt and pepper. Remove from heat.
2. In food processor, add tofu and process until very finely chopped. Add mayonnaise, curry, cilantro, and half of the mushroom mixture, leaving behind any liquid. Pour into a large bowl and add 1 cup of the bread crumbs.
3. Form into patties and coat with remaining bread crumbs.
4. Heat a large sauté pan over medium-high heat, using 1 teaspoon of oil per patty. Cook patties for 3-5 minutes or until golden brown, flip and cook for another 3-5 minutes.
5. In a small bowl, combine mayonnaise, curry, and chili sauce.
6. On each roll, spread a teaspoonful of curry mayonnaise and mango chutney. Top with a curry tofu patty.

SERVES 4

- 6 ounces button mushrooms, chopped
- ½ onion, chopped
- 1 clove garlic, chopped
- 1 tablespoon canola oil
- 1 teaspoon salt
- ½ teaspoon pepper
- 1 6-ounce package savory baked tofu
- ¾ cup vegan mayonnaise
- 2 teaspoons curry powder
- 2 tablespoons cilantro, finely chopped
- 2 cups bread crumbs
- ½ cup vegan mayonnaise
- 1 teaspoon curry
- 1 teaspoon chili sauce
- 4 sandwich rolls
- 1 jar mango chutney

Southwest Sliders with Spicy Queso Sauce

MAKES A DOZEN SLIDERS (SERVES 4)

- 1 clove garlic, minced
- ½ onion, chopped
- 1 tablespoon oil
- 4 tablespoons flour
- 2 cups nondairy milk
- 2 cups vegan Cheddar shreds
- 1 15-ounce can diced tomatoes with green chilies
- 1 jalapeño, deseeded and chopped
- ½ cup red pepper, chopped
- ½ cup onion, chopped
- ½ cup bread crumbs
- ½ cup brown rice, cooked
- ½ cup pinto beans, cooked and mashed
- ½ cup yam, cooked and mashed
- 1 teaspoon salt
- ½ teaspoon pepper
- 1 teaspoon chili powder
- 1 teaspoon cumin
- ½ teaspoon garlic powder
- Oil for frying
- Mini burger buns, or hot dog buns cut into thirds

You can buy vegan queso, but since it's such a breeze to make your own, why bother? Break out the bibs when you sit down to devour these delectable nuggets—it's a messy endeavor!

1. In a medium saucepan over medium heat, sauté garlic and onion in 1 tablespoon oil until onions are translucent. Add flour to the pan, stirring with a whisk, and cook for 1 minute. Add milk and stir until mixture thickens. Add vegan Cheddar shreds and 1 cup of diced tomatoes with chilies, drained. Bring to a boil, turn heat to low, and let simmer while burgers cook.
2. In a sauté pan over medium heat, sauté jalapeño, red peppers, and onions in oil until onions are translucent. Remove from heat.
3. In a large bowl, combine cooked onion mixture, diced tomatoes with chilies, bread crumbs, brown rice, beans, yam, salt, pepper, chili powder, cumin, and garlic powder until well mixed. Using hands, form into 3-inch patties.
4. In a large sauté or grill pan over medium-high heat, sauté burgers in a few teaspoons of oil 3-5 minutes on each side.
5. Remove Queso Sauce from heat.
6. Place cooked burgers on bottom buns and spoon Queso Sauce over patty and cover with bun top.

Buffalo Sliders with Creamy Ranch Dressing

Hit the freezer section of your favorite grocery store that carries vegan specialties to find a plethora of nuggets to use as the base of this überjunky sandwich. Don't skimp on the celery unless you want your mouth to burn off—it supplies a cool crunch to counter the five-alarm sauce.

1. In a small bowl, mix Creamy Ranch Dressing and celery.
2. In a small saucepan over medium-high heat, bring hot sauce to a boil, then remove from heat. Dip nuggets into sauce and set aside on a plate.
3. To assemble, place a heaping teaspoonful of ranch-celery mixture on the bottom bun of each sandwich. Add onion, lettuce, and tomato. Top with two nuggets and cap with bun.
4. Serve with extra ranch-celery mixture and heated hot sauce on the side.

MAKES 6 SLIDERS

- 1 recipe Creamy Ranch Dressing (see "Dips for All Seasons")
- 1 cup celery, chopped finely
- 12 vegan chicken nuggets, cooked
- 1 cup Frank's RedHot Sauce
- ½ red onion, sliced
- 1 cup lettuce, shredded
- 1 roma tomato, sliced
- 6 slider buns or hot dog buns cut into thirds

Turkey Sliders

SERVES 4

- ½ pound red potatoes, with skins, halved
- 2 tablespoons vegan margarine
- 1 teaspoon salt
- 1 teaspoon pepper
- ½ cup vegan mayonnaise
- 1 teaspoon Dijon mustard
- ¼ cup cranberry sauce, whole berry
- 1 package vegan turkey deli slices
- 6 slider rolls or hot dog buns cut into thirds

More of a holiday leftover sandwich than a traditional slider, this features mashed potatoes spread right on the bun. If that isn't the definition of comfort food, I don't know what is. Turkey + buttery potatoes + tart cranberries = a nap after lunch.

1. In a large saucepan, boil enough salted water to cover potatoes, cook for about 15 minutes or until fork-tender. Drain. Mash with margarine, salt, and pepper.
2. In a small bowl, mix mayonnaise, Dijon mustard, and cranberry sauce.
3. On each bottom roll, spread a heaping teaspoonful of the mayonnaise mixture, a heaping tablespoonful of the mashed potatoes, and two folded deli slices. Spread top of roll with extra mayonnaise, cap sandwich, and pretend it's the day after Thanksgiving.

CHAPTER 3

Comfort Food Meets Takeout

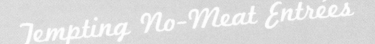

Tempting No-Meat Entrées

Chicken Potpie

SERVES 4–6

1 recipe Savory Pie Crust
½ cup carrots, diced
½ cup celery, diced
½ cup potato, diced
1 small onion, chopped
1 clove garlic, chopped
4 tablespoons vegan margarine
½ cup flour
2 cups vegetable broth
1 cup nondairy milk
½ cup nutritional yeast
½ cup frozen peas
2 vegan breaded chicken patties, chopped into 1-inch pieces
1 teaspoon celery salt
½ teaspoon pepper

The homemade Savory Pie Crust is what makes this so flipping fantastic, so resist the urge to use an inferior store-bought kind. The creamy filling that holds the goodies (a.k.a. veggies and chicken) in this epic crust tastes so rich, you may be tempted to eat it on its own by the spoonful.

1. Preheat oven to 350°F. On a lightly floured surface, roll one disk of Savory Pie Crust dough to fit into a 2-quart baking dish. Roll the other disk to fit on top.
2. In a medium sauté pan over medium-high heat, sauté carrots, celery, potato, onion, and garlic in margarine until vegetables are tender, about 10 minutes.
3. Add flour to the sautéed vegetables, then stir, cooking for 1 minute.
4. Whisk broth and milk slowly into sauté pan, cook until bubbly and thick. Add nutritional yeast, peas, chicken patties, celery salt, and pepper.
5. Pour into prepared baking dish. Top with remaining dough. Crimp edges to seal. Cut four small vent holes in top crust.
6. Bake for 45-50 minutes. Allow to cool slightly before digging in!

Savory Pie Crust

3½ cups flour
1½ teaspoons salt
2/3 cup vegan margarine, chilled
3 tablespoons olive oil
3 tablespoons ice water

1. In a food processor with the blade fitting attached, pulse flour and salt, adding margarine 1 tablespoon at a time until mixture resembles coarse meal. Alternatively, used a pastry blender or two knives to cut margarine into flour.
2. Pour in olive oil and pulse.
3. Pour in ice water a tablespoon at a time until a spoonful of dough can be formed into a ball that doesn't crumble. Do not overmix.
4. If not using immediately, wrap tightly in plastic wrap and refrigerate or freeze.

Individual Chile Potpies

It's like a Hot Pocket. But vegan. And in a pie form. And way, way better.

1. Preheat oven to 350°F. Lightly grease a six-cup muffin tray. Roll pastry on a floured surface and cut into rounds large enough to line muffin pan wells. Cut small rounds with extra dough to use as top crust.
2. In a large stockpot over medium-high heat, sauté in olive oil onion, carrot, garlic, and jalapeño. Stir occasionally until onion is translucent, about 5 minutes.
3. Add the beef crumbles and cook until browned, adding a teaspoon of oil if pan is too dry. Add chili powder, salt, and cumin and stir until very fragrant.
4. Sprinkle flour over beef crumble mixture, stirring to incorporate flour. Cook for 1 minute.
5. In a small bowl, mix the beef bouillon, water, and crushed tomatoes. Add to pan and stir constantly until it begins to thicken. Turn heat down to medium and simmer for 10 minutes.
6. Add beans and stir to heat through. Remove from heat.
7. Place a scant ¼ cup of chili into each prepared crust. Top with a round of crust.
8. Bake for 20-25 minutes until crust is golden.
9. Serve with generous side dish of Vegan Sour Cream and green onions.

SERVES 6

- 1 recipe Savory Pie Crust (see Chicken Potpie recipe)
- 1 tablespoon olive oil
- ½ onion, minced
- 1 carrot, minced
- 1 clove garlic, crushed
- 1 jalapeño pepper, deseeded, finely chopped
- 1 cup frozen vegan beef crumbles
- 1 tablespoon chili powder
- 1 teaspoon salt
- 1 teaspoon cumin
- 2 tablespoons flour
- 3 teaspoons vegan beef broth bouillon
- 2 cups water
- 1 15-ounce can crushed tomatoes
- 1 15-ounce can pinto beans
- 1 cup Vegan Sour Cream (see "Dips for All Seasons")
- ¼ cup chopped green onions

Layered Eggplant Parmesan Casserole

SERVES 6

- 1 large eggplant
- 2 cups bread crumbs
- 1 tablespoon nutritional yeast
- 1 teaspoon salt
- 1 teaspoon oregano
- 1 teaspoon parsley
- 1 cup nondairy milk
- ½ cup cornstarch
- 2 tablespoons oil for frying
- 2 cups vegan mozzarella shreds
- 1 recipe Vegan Ricotta (see "Dips for All Seasons")
- 3 cups marinara sauce

You had me at casserole. Because there's not much that's junkier than throwing everything into a big ole dish and baking it until the flavors are all melded and melty and messy and mouthwatering.

1. Preheat oven to 350°F. Lightly grease a 9" × 13" baking dish.
2. Slice eggplant into ¼-inch rounds.
3. In a shallow dish, combine bread crumbs, nutritional yeast, salt, oregano, and parsley.
4. In a second shallow dish, pour in milk.
5. In a third shallow bowl, add cornstarch.
6. In a large sauté pan over medium-high heat, heat oil.
7. Dredge each piece of eggplant in cornstarch, then milk, then coat with bread crumb mixture.
8. Fry in heated oil until golden brown on both sides, about 5-7 minutes.
9. Place cooked eggplant in a single layer in the bottom of prepared baking dish. Top with ½ cup cheese, ⅓ of the Vegan Ricotta, and 1 cup marinara. Continue layering, topping with cheese shreds.
10. Bake for 45 minutes. Let cool for 10 minutes before serving.

French Onion Soup Casserole

Who doesn't love the wall of cheese that forms the savory seal on a classic French onion soup? This version features an olive oil-drenched bread-cheese barrier that's bar none.

1. In a large sauté pan over medium-high heat, cook onions in olive oil, stirring occasionally until onions become translucent. Add salt, turn heat down to medium, and continue cooking until onions turn golden, about 15 minutes.
2. Place half of the onions in a 9" × 13" baking dish.
3. In the sauté pan, add garlic and cook for 1 minute. Sprinkle flour over onions and garlic and cook stirring constantly for 1 minute. Slowly add milk, broth, and soy sauce, stirring with a whisk. Bring to a boil and cook until it begins to slightly thicken.
4. Pour over onions in baking dish. Top with ½ cup cheese.
5. Arrange bread in baking dish, covering most of the soup. Top with remaining cheese. Cover and let sit overnight in the refrigerator or for a few hours on the counter.
6. Preheat oven to 400°F. Uncover, drizzle bread with olive oil, and bake for 30 minutes or until soup is bubbly and bread is golden.

SERVES 4

- 4 medium onions, sliced thin
- 2 tablespoons olive oil
- 1 teaspoon salt
- 1 clove garlic, chopped
- 4 tablespoons flour
- 1 cup nondairy milk
- 2 cups vegetable broth
- 2 tablespoons light soy sauce
- 1 cup vegan mozzarella shreds
- 6–8 pieces thickly sliced day-old French bread
- Olive oil

Mac and Cheese Bake

SERVES 6

- 1 recipe Cheese Sauce
  (see "Dips for All Seasons")
- ½ cup nondairy milk
- 1 pound elbow pasta, cooked
- ½ cup vegan Cheddar shreds
- ½ cup bread crumbs
- ¼ cup walnuts, finely ground
- ¼ cup nutritional yeast
- 2 tablespoons vegan
  margarine, melted

I could eat this every day of my life and die an incredibly happy woman. This is the ultimate carb-load comfort food featuring pasta, bread crumbs, vegan Cheddar shreds, nutritional yeast, margarine, and milk. It technically serves six, but if you're like me, you could easily polish off an entire recipe all by yourself.

1. Preheat oven to 350°F. Lightly grease a 9" × 13" baking dish.
2. In a large saucepan over medium heat, whisk the milk into the Cheese Sauce. When heated through, add cooked pasta, stirring to combine thoroughly.
3. Pour into prepared baking dish. Top with cheese.
4. In a small bowl, combine bread crumbs, walnuts, nutritional yeast, and margarine, and mix well. Evenly sprinkle on cheese layer.
5. Bake for 25 minutes or until top is golden brown. Waste no time devouring.

Fast Tortilla Soup

SERVES 2

- 1 cup vegetable broth
- 2 tablespoons instant rice
- 1 teaspoon vegan chicken
  bouillon
- ¼ teaspoon onion powder
- ⅛ teaspoon garlic powder
- ⅛ teaspoon cumin
- 1 tablespoon nutritional yeast
- ¼ cup tortilla chips, crushed

Adding tortilla chips to any dish automatically qualifies it as junk food. And there are a million different tortilla chip varieties to choose from. In this vegan quickie, feel free to experiment. Heck, even Spicy Sweet Chili-flavored Doritos would do the trick!

1. In a small saucepan over medium-high heat, bring vegetable broth to a boil. Stir in rice, chicken bouillon, onion powder, garlic powder, and cumin; stir. Cook for 5 minutes or until rice is tender.
2. Pour soup into a bowl and top with nutritional yeast and tortilla chips.

Chile Rellenos Casserole

Adding vinegar to soymilk is a vegan trick for creating a "sour" milk (similar to the tangy flavor of buttermilk). For a taste of Mexico, this recipe satisfies—serve with a piping hot side of Tex-Mex Corn Bread (see "Crusts and Carbs").

1. Preheat oven to 375°F. Lightly grease a 9" x 9" baking dish.
2. In a small bowl, mix soymilk and apple cider vinegar, then set aside.
3. In a medium bowl, mix cream cheese and cheese shreds until well combined. Make a small slit at the top of each chili and stuff with ⅛ of the cheese filling. Lay stuffed chilies in prepared baking dish.
4. In a medium bowl with a whisk, stir flour, nutritional yeast, baking soda, baking powder, salt, and turmeric. Stir in soymilk-vinegar mixture. Pour into a blender and mix on high speed for 1 minute.
5. Pour over chilies.
6. Bake for 25 minutes or until batter is set and golden brown. *Buen provecho!*

SERVES 4

- 1 cup soymilk
- 1 teaspoon apple cider vinegar
- 1 8-ounce container vegan cream cheese
- 4 cups vegan Cheddar shreds
- 8 canned whole green chilies, drained and rinsed
- 1 cup flour
- 3 tablespoons nutritional yeast
- 1½ teaspoons baking soda
- 2 teaspoons baking powder
- ½ teaspoon salt
- ⅛ teaspoon turmeric

Carne Asada Tacos

SERVES 6

3 cups vegetable broth

2 teaspoons vegan beef bouillon paste

1 cup chunk-style or large-cube textured vegetable protein

2 tablespoons oil

½ cup onion, chopped

1 tablespoon vegan Worcestershire sauce

1 teaspoon salt

½ teaspoon pepper

1 small onion, chopped

¼ cup cilantro, chopped

12 corn tortillas

1 recipe Avocado Sauce (see "Dips for All Seasons")

This vegan street taco features chunks of TVP sautéed with onion until it's deep golden brown and oh-so-flavorful. Worcestershire sauce is the secret ingredient that gives this a salty-meaty kick. Finish by drizzling (or drenching) with creamy-cooling Avocado Sauce.

1. In a saucepan over high heat, bring vegetable broth, beef bouillon, and TVP chunks to a boil. Cook until pieces are tender all the way through, about 5 minutes. Drain well. Place chunks in a clean kitchen towel and squeeze excess water out.
2. In a medium sauté pan over medium high, heat oil and sauté onion until golden brown. Add TVP chunks and cook for 8–10 minutes, adding more oil if needed to keep from sticking. Brown TVP on all sides. Add Worcestershire sauce, salt, and pepper to pan and cook for 2 more minutes. Remove from heat.
3. In a small bowl, mix onion and cilantro.
4. In a dry sauté pan over medium heat, cook corn tortillas just until they turn soft, about 30 seconds on each side, and keep wrapped in a towel.
5. Spoon a heaping tablespoonful of Carne Asada onto each tortilla; add a teaspoonful of onion-cilantro mixture.
6. Serve with Avocado Sauce.

South-of-the-Border Potato Tacos

A cheesy, caliente potato taco is delicious. A cheesy, caliente potato taco that's fried is outta this world. Creamy Avocado Sauce is served on the side (better just make a *really* big batch).

1. In a medium pot, boil potatoes in 1 teaspoon salt until tender, then drain.
2. In a medium sauté pan over medium-high heat, cook onions and jalapeño in oil until onion is translucent, then add cumin.
3. Turn heat down to low and add potatoes, 1 teaspoon salt, cilantro, nutritional yeast, and cheese. Mash potatoes slightly, stirring to combine all ingredients. Cook for 2-3 minutes. Remove from heat.
4. In a dry skillet over medium-high heat, place tortillas in the pan one at a time heating on each side a few seconds, just long enough to soften. Wrap in a kitchen towel to keep warm.
5. Fill each tortilla with 2 heaping tablespoonfuls of potato mixture and fold.
6. Add 1 tablespoon oil to pan and cook each tortilla on each side until crispy.
7. Serve with Avocado Sauce on the side.

SERVES 3–4

- 1 pound baking potatoes, peeled and chopped into 2-inch pieces
- 2 teaspoons salt, divided
- ¼ cup onion, diced
- 1 jalapeño, seeded and chopped finely
- 1 teaspoon cumin
- 2 teaspoons oil
- ¼ cup cilantro, chopped
- ¼ cup nutritional yeast
- ½ cup vegan mozzarella shreds
- 6 corn tortillas
- 1 recipe Avocado Sauce (see "Dips for All Seasons")

Tempeh Fajitas

1 tablespoon flour

1–2 teaspoons chili powder

1 teaspoon salt

1 teaspoon garlic powder

1 teaspoon minced onion

1 teaspoon ground cumin

1 teaspoon salt

¼ cup lime juice

1 tablespoon olive oil

1 8-ounce package tempeh,
  cut into ¼-inch slices

1–2 teaspoons olive oil

1 medium onion, sliced thin

1 red or green bell pepper,
  sliced thin

¼ cup cilantro, finely chopped

1 ripe avocado, sliced

1 recipe Easy Salsa Fresca
  (see "Dips for All Seasons")

4 10-inch flour tortillas

Break out the grill pan, folks. It's time to make fajitas. Delectable breaded tempeh fajitas at that. The Easy Salsa Fresca is pretty healthy and tastes great as a topping, but if you're on a true junk food bender, I understand if you opt to omit.

1. In a small shallow dish, mix flour, chili powder, salt, garlic powder, onion, cumin, salt, lime juice, and oil. Add tempeh, turning to coat, and let marinate for at least 1 hour.
2. In a large grill pan or sauté pan over medium-high heat, cook onions and peppers in 1 teaspoon of olive oil until onions are charred on one side, about 5 minutes in the grill pan or sauté until golden and tender crisp. Remove the peppers and onions to a serving plate. Add the tempeh and 1 teaspoon of olive oil. Cook until tempeh becomes slightly crispy and browned. Place on serving plate with peppers and onions.
3. In a dry skillet over medium-high heat, warm each tortilla until soft and wrap in a kitchen towel to keep the stack warm.
4. Place tempeh and peppers in warm tortillas and garnish with cilantro, avocado, and Easy Salsa Fresca.

Black Bean and Cheese Empanadas

Ooooooh, empanadas! If you're a fan of Mexican food, you need to learn how to make these now, so please drop everything and start gathering the ingredients. Once you take your first rich, flaky, savory, cheesy bite, you'll know it was all worth it.

1. In large sauté pan over medium-high heat, pour in olive oil and sauté zucchini and onions until onion is translucent. Then stir in tomato paste, cumin, salt, and pepper. Add black beans and stir, mashing beans slightly. Remove from heat. Stir in cheese. Set aside.
2. In a food processor, pulse together flour, baking powder, and salt.
3. Drop in shortening 1 tablespoon at a time. If doing by hand, use two knives or a pastry cutter. Pulse or mix by hand until mixture looks like coarse crumbs.
4. Mix water and vinegar. Add to dough mixture 1 tablespoon at a time, pulsing after each addition until a tablespoonful of dough holds together when pressed into a ball. Do not overmix.
5. Roll dough into a large ball, then divide into 16 balls. Cover and refrigerate for at least 1 hour.
6. Preheat oven to 375°F. Line a baking sheet with parchment paper.
7. On a floured surface, roll each dough ball out to ⅛-inch thickness.
8. Spoon 2 tablespoons of bean mixture on each dough round. Brush the edge of dough with water and fold in half. Crimp edges shut by hand or with a fork, sealing in filling.
9. Bake for 20 minutes or until golden brown. Serve with Avocado Sauce.

SERVES 4–6

- 1 tablespoon oil
- 1 cup zucchini, finely chopped
- 1 small onion, minced
- 1 tablespoon tomato paste
- 1 teaspoon cumin
- 1 teaspoon salt
- ½ teaspoon pepper
- 1 15-ounce can black beans, drained and rinsed
- ½ cup vegan mozzarella shreds
- 2½ cups flour
- 1 teaspoon baking powder
- 1 teaspoon salt
- ½ cup vegan nonhydrogenated shortening, chilled
- ½ cup ice water
- 1 tablespoon vinegar
- 1 recipe Avocado Sauce (see "Dips for All Seasons")

Linguine Creamy Garlic Alfredo with Peas and Bacon

SERVES 4

- 1 teaspoon olive oil
- 2 cloves garlic, chopped
- 1 cup soy creamer
- 1 8-ounce package vegan cream cheese, softened
- 2 tablespoons nutritional yeast
- 1 tablespoon vegan bacon bits
- 1 cup frozen peas
- 1 teaspoon salt
- ½ teaspoon pepper
- 1 16-ounce package linguine, cooked according to package directions
- 1 tablespoon vegan margarine
- 2 tablespoons fresh parsley, chopped

Faux bacon bits (I like Frontier's Bac'Uns) rank up there as one of the best foodstuff inventions for vegans. After eating this rich, creamy recipe, you'll think you ordered off the menu at Olive Garden.

1. In a medium sauté pan over medium-high heat, cook garlic until very fragrant in olive oil, about 2 minutes.
2. Turn the heat down to low and mix in soy creamer. Add the cream cheese and stir using a whisk to combine well.
3. Mix in nutritional yeast, bacon bits, peas, salt, and pepper, stirring constantly; do not let the mixture boil. Cook for 5 minutes or until sauce is steaming and peas are cooked.
4. In a large serving bowl, toss the cooked pasta with margarine and parsley.
5. Pour sauce over pasta. Serve with Ranch Garlic Bread (see "Crusts and Carbs").

Chicken-Fried Seitan and Gravy

Remember Shake 'n Bake chicken? Here's the vegan version.
Bonus: You can drown your deep-fried seitan in a decadent,
artery-clogging gravy. Yum!

1. In a medium bowl, mix milk and apple cider vinegar. Let sit 5 minutes.
2. In a large skillet, heat 2 inches of oil to 375°F or until bubbles appear around a chopstick when placed in oil.
3. In a 1-gallon plastic zippered storage bag, add flour, salt, and pepper.
4. Dip each seitan piece into milk mixture, then place in flour bag and shake to coat.
5. Fry each piece about 3-4 minutes or until golden brown on each side.
6. Drain on paper towels.

Gravy

1. In a medium sauté pan over medium heat, melt the margarine; when bubbly, whisk in flour and stir, cooking for 1 minute. Slowly add the chicken broth and milk, stirring constantly until gravy is thick. Season with salt and pepper.
2. Serve hot over Chicken-Fried Seitan.

SERVES 4

- 2 cups soymilk
- 2 tablespoons apple cider vinegar
- 1 cup self-rising flour
- ½ teaspoon salt
- ½ teaspoon pepper
- 1 8-ounce package seitan strips

- 2 tablespoons vegan margarine
- 2 tablespoons flour
- 1 cup vegan chicken broth
- 1 cup soy creamer or nondairy milk
- 1 teaspoon salt
- 1 teaspoon pepper

Mushroom Stroganoff

SERVES 4

- 1 pound portobello mushrooms, cut into ¼-inch slices
- 2 tablespoons olive oil
- 1 medium onion, chopped
- 1 6-ounce package button mushrooms, chopped
- 1 teaspoon salt
- 1 pound fettuccine or pasta noodle of choice
- 1 cup vegetable broth
- 2 tablespoons cognac (optional)
- 1 tablespoon vegan margarine, melted
- 1 tablespoon chopped fresh parsley
- 1 cup Vegan Sour Cream (see "Dips for All Seasons")

Rich doesn't begin to describe the flavor profile of this hearty and filling pasta dish. It's perennially popular among my catering clients as well as my family. Serve with a generous basket of Ranch Garlic Bread (see "Crusts and Carbs") and sit back and accept the compliments to the chef.

1. In a 4-quart pot, bring 2 quarts of water to a boil.
2. In a large sauté pan over medium-high heat, cook portobello mushrooms in small batches in a few teaspoons of olive oil. Let mushrooms slightly brown and remove from pan; cook next batch adding oil a teaspoon at a time when needed. Set aside.
3. Add onions to the pan and cook until translucent and beginning to turn golden, about 5 minutes.
4. Add button mushrooms to pan and salt. Use another teaspoon of oil if the pan is too dry. Cook the mushrooms for 10 minutes, stirring occasionally.
5. Put pasta in boiling water. Cook for time indicated on package during the next step.
6. Add the vegetable broth and cognac to the button mushrooms. Cook for 10-15 minutes until liquid has reduced and can coat the back of a spoon.
7. Place pasta in a large serving dish. Toss with 1 tablespoon vegan margarine and chopped parsley.
8. Lower the heat on the mushroom mixture and stir in sour cream. Bring just to a simmer and add the portobello mushrooms back to pan, stirring to heat through.
9. Pour stroganoff over pasta and get busy eating.

Savory Twice-Baked Potatoes

Better than French fries or potato skins, these spuds are baked and mixed with cream cheese, sour cream, margarine, chives, cheese, and bacon, then baked again until the filling is molten and fluffy.

1. Preheat oven to 350°F.
2. With a fork, poke each potato 4 or 5 times to release steam as it cooks. Place in the oven directly on the middle rack. Bake for 1 hour.
3. Remove from oven and, holding with an oven mitt, slice each in half. Set on counter to cool.
4. Line a baking sheet with parchment paper.
5. In a large bowl, scoop out baked potato leaving a ¼-inch shell.
6. In a medium bowl with a whisk, cream together cream cheese, sour cream, and margarine.
7. Spoon the cream cheese mixture into the potatoes, using a masher to incorporate well. Add salt, pepper, garlic, chives, nutritional yeast, 1 cup Cheddar shreds, and bacon bits.
8. Stuff each baked potato shell with heaping tablespoonfuls of filling. Place on prepared baking sheet.
9. Sprinkle remaining ½ cup Cheddar shreds and paprika on top.
10. Bake for 20 minutes and eat while piping hot.

SERVES 4

- 4 baking potatoes, scrubbed
- 1 8-ounce container vegan cream cheese
- 1 cup vegan sour cream
- 3 tablespoons vegan margarine
- 1 teaspoon salt
- ½ teaspoon pepper
- 1 clove garlic, crushed
- 2 tablespoons chives, finely chopped
- ½ cup nutritional yeast
- 1½ cups vegan Cheddar shreds
- 2 tablespoons vegan bacon bits
- 2 teaspoons paprika

Corn Dogs with a Tangy Mustard Dipping Sauce

SERVES 6

Oil for frying
1 cup soymilk
1 tablespoon apple cider vinegar
1 cup Bisquick
½ cup cornmeal
1 teaspoon seasoned salt
¼ onion, grated
1 package vegan hot dogs
6 popsicle sticks or chopsticks
4 tablespoons flour

A vegan version of the carnival classic that you can make at home in a pinch. Need I say more?

1. Prepare deep fryer according to directions or heat 4 inches of oil in a heavy pot to 375°F.
2. In a small bowl, add the soymilk and apple cider vinegar, then set aside.
3. In a medium bowl, stir together Bisquick, cornmeal, and seasoned salt.
4. Add soymilk-vinegar mixture and onion to dry ingredients and stir just until combined.
5. In a drinking glass, pour in batter until it is about ¾ full.
6. Prepare hot dogs by placing a stick in each dog and rolling in flour.
7. When oil is ready, dip each floured hot dog into the drinking glass full of batter.
8. Wearing an oven mitt, place battered hot dog into heated oil, holding the stick carefully, and cook for 4-6 minutes or until very golden brown.
9. Serve with tangy mustard sauce.

Mustard Sauce

½ cup Dijon mustard
¼ cup vegan mayonnaise
¼ cup agave
1 tablespoon apple cider vinegar

1. In a small bowl, mix mustard, mayonnaise, agave, and vinegar with a whisk until very well combined.

Tortilla Chip Soup

There's a quick version of this soup that appears earlier in the book, but this is a heartier version for those with bigger appetites. Ramp up the amount of tortilla chips added to the soup according to your hankering for salt and crunch.

1. In a medium sauté pan over medium-high heat, sauté in olive oil celery, onion, corn, garlic, and jalapeño. Cook until onion is translucent, about 5 minutes. Add salt, pepper, and cumin; stir until cumin becomes very fragrant, about 1 minute.
2. Add vegetable broth and tomatoes. Bring to a boil, turn heat down to medium, and simmer for 10 minutes. Remove from heat and stir in lime juice.
3. Ladle soup into bowls, garnish with cilantro and avocado slices, and top with tortilla chips.

SERVES 4

- 1 tablespoon olive oil
- ½ cup chopped celery
- ½ cup chopped onion
- ½ cup corn, fresh-cut from cob
- 1 clove garlic, chopped
- 1 jalapeño, seeded and chopped
- 1 teaspoon salt
- ½ teaspoon pepper
- 2 teaspoons cumin
- 6 cups vegetable broth
- 2 medium tomatoes, seeded and chopped
- 3 tablespoons lime juice
- ¼ cup cilantro, finely chopped
- 1 ripe avocado, sliced
  Tortilla chips

Italian Sausage and Peppers with Vodka Marinara

SERVES 4

1 red bell pepper, sliced
1 green bell pepper, sliced
1 onion, sliced
1 tablespoon oil
1 14-ounce package vegan Italian sausage
1 6-ounce package button mushrooms, chopped
½ cup vodka
6 cups marinara
   Oil for frying

For a quick and dirty dinner with a spicy kick, this is your answer. Vegan sausage is widely available, so be sure to test out lots of varieties before arriving at your favorite.

1. In a large sauté pan over medium-high heat, sauté peppers and onions in oil. Cook until onions are translucent and tender. Remove from heat. Add sausages to the pan and cook until browned on all sides, adding oil if needed to prevent sticking. Remove from pan.
2. Add mushrooms to the pan and sauté until they begin to slightly brown, 5-7 minutes.
3. Pour vodka into pan and stir; cook for about 1 minute.
4. Pour marinara over vodka and bring to a boil. Lower heat to medium and cook for 10 minutes.
5. Add peppers and sausages back to pan and heat through, about 5 minutes.

Beer Brat–Stuffed Portobello Mushrooms with Steak Fries

So satisfying and filling, these portobellos are jammed with a creamy, cheesy beer brat mixture and baked. As if that weren't enough, they're served with a plate full of fries for the ultimate vegan meat-and-potatoes meal.

1. Preheat oven to 350°F. Line a baking sheet with parchment paper. (If making steak fries, start cooking those first.)
2. Remove stems from portobello mushrooms, discard any tough parts, finely chop the remaining stem pieces, and set aside. Place whole mushrooms on prepared baking sheet. (Put the steak fries in oven while you do this.)
3. In a large bowl, mix cream cheese and margarine until well combined, then add bread crumbs, walnuts, nutritional yeast, parsley, salt, and pepper.
4. In a medium sauté pan over medium-high heat, sauté beer brats, onion, mushrooms, and garlic in olive oil until onions are translucent, about 6 minutes. Remove from heat.
5. Add the beer brat mixture to the cream cheese and mix to combine.
6. Spoon into mushrooms, dividing evenly.
7. Bake for 25 minutes. Serve with steak fries.

SERVES 4

- 4 portobello mushrooms
- 1 8-ounce container vegan cream cheese, softened
- 2 tablespoons vegan margarine, softened
- 2 cups bread crumbs
- ¼ cup walnuts, finely ground
- ¼ cup nutritional yeast
- 2 teaspoons parsley
- 1 teaspoon salt
- ½ teaspoon pepper
- 2 Tofurky Beer Brats, cut into 1-inch pieces
- 1 medium onion, chopped
- 1 clove garlic, chopped
- 1 tablespoon olive oil

Steak Fries

1. Preheat oven to 350°F. Line a baking sheet with parchment paper.
2. Peel and cut potatoes into planks about ¼-inch thick.
3. In a large bowl, toss potatoes with olive oil and garlic salt, coating well.
4. Place in a single layer on prepared baking sheet.
5. Bake for 35-40 minutes.
6. Serve with Garlic Chive Dip.

- 1 pound baking potatoes
- 2 tablespoons olive oil
- 1 teaspoon garlic salt
- 1 recipe Garlic Chive Dip (See "Dips for All Seasons")

Mongolian Beef

SERVES 4

1 9-ounce package Gardein vegan beefless tips or 1 8-ounce package of tempeh

4 tablespoons cornstarch

1 teaspoon oil

2 cloves garlic, crushed

½ teaspoon ginger

½ teaspoon red pepper flakes

½ cup light soy sauce

¼ cup brown sugar

1 tablespoon oil

1 carrot, cut into long, thin noodle-like strips

1 green onion, chopped on the diagonal

Cows everywhere do a little dance when they see a recipe like this, which features protein that's kinder and gentler but still tastes like the real deal. Gingery-garlicky goodness is the result of this superquick stir-fry.

1. In a shallow dish, dredge beef strips in the cornstarch and set aside.
2. In a medium sauté pan over medium-high heat, heat the oil, then add garlic and ginger, cooking until very fragrant, 1 or 2 minutes. Add the red pepper flakes. Pour in soy sauce and whisk in sugar. Sauce will slightly thicken as it simmers, about 3 minutes. Remove from heat and transfer sauce to a bowl. Wipe out pan.
3. In the same pan over high heat, sauté the beef strips and carrots in 1 tablespoon oil until carrots are tender-crisp, about 5 minutes. Pour sauce into the pan and cook for an additional 2 minutes, remove from heat, and stir in green onion.
4. Serve over rice.

Noodles with Tofu and Cashew Stir-Fry

If you wanted to start your own vegan Asian takeout, this would be a recipe to include under "House Specials." Take out your wok and give it a spin—you get all the classic noodle house flavors and it stir-fries up in a snap!

1. In a medium bowl, toss tofu and cornstarch. Remove tofu, shaking off excess cornstarch.
2. In a large sauté pan (or wok) over medium-high heat, sauté tofu in oil until golden brown. Remove tofu from pan. In the same pan, sauté red chili pepper, garlic, ginger, cashews, and snow peas until very fragrant, about 1 minute.
3. Add hoisin, light soy sauce, brown sugar, vinegar, and water, and stir to combine. Add tofu back to the pan and stir in noodles. Use tongs to mix noodles into sauce.
4. Remove from heat and serve. Don't forget the chopsticks!

SERVES 4

- 1 16-ounce container firm tofu, drained, diced into 1-inch cubes
- ½ cup cornstarch
- 2 tablespoons oil
- 1 red chili pepper, sliced
- 2 cloves garlic, chopped
- 1 teaspoon ginger, grated
- 1 cup cashews
- 1 cup snow peas, halved
- ¼ cup hoisin
- ¼ cup light soy sauce
- 2 tablespoons brown sugar
- 3 tablespoons seasoned rice vinegar
- ¼ cup water
- 6 ounces lo mein noodles, cooked and drained
- Oil for sautéing

Spring Rolls

SERVES 4–6

6 ounces savory baked tofu, cut into long, thin pieces
1 carrot, julienned or grated
1 cup cooked glass noodles
½ cup bean sprouts
¼ cup cilantro, finely chopped
¼ cup basil leaves
¼ teaspoon sesame oil
1 tablespoon hoisin
6 spring roll rice papers

Raw or fried, these vegan goodies are an essential addition to any Asian feast. Unlike the takeout varieties, which are invariably limp, cold, and sad, these will remain fresh and/or warm-crispy. The Wasabi Soy and Spicy Peanut dipping sauces make them even more awesome.

1. In a medium bowl, mix tofu, carrot, noodles, bean sprouts, cilantro, and basil. Add sesame oil and hoisin, and toss to coat evenly.
2. Fill a shallow dish halfway with water. Place one rice paper at a time, allowing to soak in water for about 6 seconds or just until pliable. Let water drip off.
3. Spoon about 2 heaping tablespoonfuls of filling onto wrapper. Fold the bottom up about ¼ of the way over filling, fold in each side, and then continue rolling toward the top edge.
4. Serve spring rolls with Wasabi Soy Dipping Sauce (see "Dips for All Seasons").

Crispy Fried Spring Rolls

1. Prepare Spring Rolls as directed above.
2. Heat about 3 inches of oil in a frying pan over medium-high heat. Heat oil to 375°F or until bubbles appear around a chopstick when inserted in oil.
3. Carefully place spring rolls in oil two at a time depending on the size of the pan. Fry on each side until golden brown, about 3-5 minutes.
4. Place on paper towels.
5. Serve with Spicy Peanut Sauce (see "Dips for All Seasons").

Takeout Orange Tofu

Ever wonder what was in that orange sauce that bathes the tofu from Mr. Chang's Dynasty? Mystery solved.

1. In a medium saucepan over medium-high heat, combine 1 cup water, orange zest, orange juice, lemon juice, vinegar, soy sauce, brown sugar, pepper flakes, ginger, and garlic. Bring to a boil, stirring occasionally.
2. In a small bowl, whisk together cornstarch and ½ cup water. Add to the saucepan. Bring back to a boil, then turn heat down to medium-low; cook until sauce has thickened, about 5 minutes. Remove from heat.
3. In a shallow dish, stir together flour, salt, and pepper, then add tofu and stir to coat all pieces in flour mixture.
4. In a large sauté pan over medium-high heat, add about 2 tablespoons of oil. Cook the tofu in batches, frying until golden and very crispy on each side. Drain on paper towels.
5. Add tofu to sauce and stir in green onions. Serve immediately.

SERVES 4

- 1 cup water
- Zest of 1 orange
- 2 tablespoons orange juice
- 3 tablespoons lemon juice
- ½ cup rice wine vinegar
- 3 tablespoons light soy sauce
- ¾ cup brown sugar
- ¼ teaspoon red pepper flakes
- ½ teaspoon grated ginger
- 1 clove garlic, crushed
- 2 tablespoons cornstarch
- ½ cup water
- ½ cup flour
- 1 teaspoon salt
- ½ teaspoon pepper
- 1 16-ounce package firm tofu, drained, cut into 1-inch pieces
- Oil for frying
- 2 green onions, chopped on the diagonal

Takeout Fried Rice

SERVES 4

- 1 tablespoon sesame seeds
- 2 tablespoons vegan margarine
- 1 cup peas, thawed (if frozen), blanched (if fresh)
- 2 carrots, diced and blanched
- 4 cups cooked brown rice, at room temperature
- 3 tablespoons soy sauce

The Chinese food industry really doesn't want the curtain pulled back on how to make fried rice because it's so ridiculously easy that if folks knew how to make it at home, they might never order it from a restaurant again. In an effort to get your junk food even faster, here's how it's done.

1. In a large sauté pan over high heat, add sesame seeds to dry pan and stir constantly until seeds turn light golden brown, then remove from pan.
2. Add margarine to pan. When melted completely and bubbly, stir in peas, carrots, and rice. Stir constantly while adding soy sauce. Cook for about 5 minutes.
3. Transfer to a serving dish and stir in sesame seeds.

Won Ton Samosas

When you can't decide between Indian and Asian for dinner, look to this dish to satisfy your craving for fusion food. Of course, this is deep-fried, so it falls squarely in the category of fusion *junk* food, but that doesn't mean we love it any less. (In fact, it's just the opposite.)

1. In a medium sauté pan over medium-high heat, sauté the cumin seeds in oil until fragrant, about 1 minute. Turn heat down to medium; add the potatoes and garlic and cover. Cook for about 10 minutes, stirring occasionally. Add salt, turmeric, peas, and water and stir. Cover and cook until water is absorbed and potatoes are tender, adding more water a few tablespoons at a time if necessary to cook potatoes. Remove from heat.
2. Heat about 3 inches of oil in a deep sauté pan to 360°F.
3. On each won ton wrapper, wet the edges with water, place a heaping teaspoonful of filling in the middle, and fold into a triangle, sealing in filling by crimping edges with a fork.
4. Fry each won ton in oil about 2-3 minutes, turning until each side is golden brown. Drain on paper towels.
5. Stir tamarind paste, if using, into Spicy Peanut Sauce. Serve.

SERVES 4–6

- 2 tablespoons oil
- ½ teaspoon cumin seeds
- 1 pound potatoes, peeled and chopped into ½-inch cubes
- 2 cloves garlic
- 1 teaspoon salt
- ½ teaspoon turmeric
- ½ cup peas
- 1/3 cup water
- ¼ cup cilantro, finely chopped
- 1 package vegan won ton wrappers
- 1 recipe Spicy Peanut Sauce (see "Dips for All Seasons")
- 2 teaspoons tamarind paste (optional)

Tofu Eggplant Tikka Masala

SERVES 4

1 cup vegan unsweetened soygurt

3 teaspoons tikka masala spice blend

1 teaspoon ginger, grated

1 clove garlic, chopped

1 teaspoon salt

1 16-ounce package extra-firm tofu, drained

1 large eggplant

1 tablespoon olive oil

1 onion, diced

1 medium tomato, seeded and diced

1 cup frozen peas

1 tablespoon cilantro, finely chopped

1 tablespoon lemon juice

We don't need no stinking yogurt, especially when there's soygurt! And with that, we can create the creamy Indian classic that is tikka masala. If you're looking for a meatier rendition, sub out the tofu with a vegan meat product.

1. In a large bowl, whisk the soygurt, tikka masala, ginger, garlic, and salt.
2. Cut tofu and eggplant into 1-inch dices. Add to the soygurt marinade and let sit at least 1 hour.
3. In a large sauté pan over medium heat, sauté onion in olive oil until translucent. Add tomatoes to the pan and cook until they begin to break down, about 4 minutes.
4. Add the marinated tofu and eggplant to the sauté pan with marinade. Cook until eggplant is tender, being careful not to break up tofu too much, about 10 minutes.
5. Stir in peas and heat through. Taste to see if it needs more tikka masala spice. Add 1 teaspoon at a time to desired heat. Remove from heat.
6. Stir in cilantro and lemon juice.

CHAPTER 4

Crusts and Carbs

*Pizza Pies and
Badass Breads*

Basic Pizza Dough

1 cup warm water*

1 package active dry yeast

3 cups flour

1 teaspoon salt

3 tablespoons olive oil

You can find vegan pizza dough at your favorite grocery that stocks products that are kind to animals and the planet, but if time allows, give this homemade dough a whirl. It's easy enough and awfully tasty.

1. In a small bowl, mix water and yeast.
2. In a large bowl, mix flour and salt, make a well in the center, and pour in water/yeast mixture and olive oil.
3. Mix with a wooden spoon or dough hook in a mixer until mixture forms a ball.
4. Turn out onto a floured board and knead for 5 minutes. Transfer to a greased bowl and let the dough rise in a warm place for 90 minutes.
5. Divide dough into number of pizzas desired. Place dough on a floured surface and roll dough out to desired size or shape by hand. Place dough on a baking sheet liberally coated with cornmeal, or on a pizza pan.
6. Add desired toppings and bake at 425°F for 20-25 minutes.

*when poured across wrist, it should feel slightly warmer than body temperature

Super-Easy Pizza Sauce

There's nothing like fresh marinara. The jarred stuff is always a little questionable, a little too acidic with limp herbs and *never* enough garlic. Although this isn't technically 100 percent "fresh," it comes a helluva lot closer than the alternative and is simple to prep. Do yourself a favor and make a few batches to have on hand for when a pizza craving strikes.

1. In a large bowl, mix all the ingredients together and allow to sit for at least 1 hour before using for flavors to marry. You will need roughly ½ cup of sauce per 12-inch pizza. Leftover sauce is also great on pasta.

MAKES 2½ CUPS

- 2 cups crushed tomatoes
- 1 6-ounce can tomato paste
- ¼ cup nutritional yeast
- 2 tablespoons sugar
- 1 teaspoon dried basil, or 1 tablespoon fresh, chopped fine
- 1 teaspoon dried oregano, or 2 teaspoons fresh, chopped fine
- ¼ teaspoon marjoram
- ¼ teaspoon pepper
- 1–2 cloves garlic, crushed

Tandoori Tempeh Pizza on Onion-Garlic Naan

SERVES 4

1 6-ounce carton plain unsweetened soygurt

2 tablespoons lemon juice

2 garlic cloves, minced

1 teaspoon fresh ginger, grated

1 teaspoon salt

1 teaspoon cumin

1 teaspoon coriander

1 teaspoon chili powder (optional)

½ teaspoon paprika

½ teaspoon turmeric

1 8-ounce package tempeh, chopped into 2-inch cubes

½ recipe Onion-Garlic Naan (see recipe later in this chapter) or 6 whole-wheat pitas

¼ onion, sliced thin

1 6-ounce carton plain unsweetened soygurt

1 medium cucumber, peeled, seeded, chopped fine or grated

1 tablespoon lemon juice

2 teaspoons fresh mint leaves, chopped

½ teaspoon sugar

½ teaspoon salt

A super-flavorful pizza with an Indian flair, featuring warming spices and a cool cucumber dip. This reminds me of something you could order at a small out-of-the-way Indian eatery in London . . . best enjoyed at 2 A.M. after consuming many pints.

1. In a large shallow dish, add soygurt, lemon juice, garlic, ginger, salt, cumin, coriander, chili powder, paprika, and turmeric, using a whisk to combine. Add tempeh and marinate overnight for best results.
2. Preheat oven to 500°F. Line a cookie sheet with parchment paper.
3. Place cooked naan on cookie sheet. Top with marinated tempeh and onions. Drizzle with olive oil.
4. Place sheet under the broiler and broil for 4-6 minutes watching carefully. Tempeh and onions should brown and naan should crisp but not burn.
5. Serve with Cucumber Soygurt Sauce.

Cucumber Soygurt Sauce

1. In a medium bowl, mix together soygurt, cucumber, lemon juice, mint, sugar, and salt.
2. Keep refrigerated; use within 3 days.

Baked Ziti Pizza

If you thought pasta alone was a filling meal, try topping a pizza with it! You don't need to be running a marathon to enjoy this ultimate carb-load treat featuring three kinds of cheese and a delectable crusty texture.

1. Preheat oven to 475°F. Place rolled or stretched Basic Pizza Dough on a prepared 16-inch pizza pan or a greased and cornmeal-sprinkled cookie sheet.
2. Spread ½ cup Super-Easy Pizza Sauce on dough evenly. Top with spoonfuls of Vegan Ricotta, spreading out into a thin layer over sauce.
3. In a large bowl, toss together ziti, 1 cup Super-Easy Pizza Sauce, oil, and ½ cup cheese shreds.
4. In a small bowl, mix ground walnuts, 1 teaspoon oil, nutritional yeast, and a pinch of salt (this will be the Parmesan).
5. Pour ziti mixture on sauce layer. Top with Parmesan mixture and cheese shreds. Cut a piece of foil to cover ziti, leaving crust uncovered.
6. Bake for 20-25 minutes, removing foil for the last 5 minutes.

SERVES 4

- 1 recipe of Basic Pizza Dough, uncooked (see recipe earlier in this chapter)
- 1½ cups Super-Easy Pizza Sauce (also in this chapter)
- 1 cup Vegan Ricotta (see "Dips for All Seasons")
- 3 cups cooked ziti pasta
- 1 tablespoon oil
- ½ cup walnuts, ground
- ¼ cup nutritional yeast
- 1 teaspoon oil
- 1½ cups vegan mozzarella shreds
  Pinch of salt

Spicy Onion and Sausage Pizza

SERVES 4

1 recipe of Basic Pizza Dough, uncooked

¾ cup Super-Easy Pizza Sauce

1–2 teaspoons dried crushed red chili flakes, depending on how spicy you want it

1 14-ounce tube Gimme Lean Sausage, pulled apart into 1-inch chunks

1 medium onion, sliced thin

2 teaspoons olive oil

1 cup vegan mozzarella shreds

Make like you are in Little Italy and serve this up to your omnivorous friends. Break out your best Italian accent and really give 'em a show! For the finale, let them know what they just ate was pig-friendly and see the look of shock when it dawns on them they just ate a vegan sausage pizza. Then expect a few converts.

1. Preheat oven to 475°F. Place rolled or stretched dough on a prepared 16-inch pizza pan or a greased and cornmeal-sprinkled cookie sheet.
2. In a sauté pan, cook the sausage chunks and red chili flakes in olive oil until browned on all sides. Remove from heat.
3. Pour pizza sauce over dough and spread evenly, followed with sausage and onions. Top with cheese.
4. Bake for 20-25 minutes.

Meatball Pizza with Peppers and Onions

Don't like bell peppers? Add more onions. Not an onion fan? Add more meatballs. Don't like sauce? Well, I can't help you there, but you get the idea. You can make pizza recipes your own by ramping up the toppings that speak to your deepest foodie desires.

1. Preheat oven to 475°F. Place rolled or stretched dough on a prepared 16-inch pizza pan or a greased and cornmeal-sprinkled cookie sheet.
2. In a large sauté pan over medium-high heat, cook onions and peppers in olive oil until tender, about 6 minutes. Add garlic and cook for 1 more minute.
3. Pour pizza sauce over dough and spread evenly, followed with meatballs, peppers, and onions. Top with cheese.
4. Bake for 20-25 minutes. Slice and enjoy!

SERVES 4

- 1 recipe of Basic Pizza Dough, uncooked
- ¾ cup Super-Easy Pizza Sauce
- 1 recipe Meatballs (see Meatball Subwich in "Deli Favorites")
  or
- 1 12-ounce package frozen vegan meatballs
- 1 medium onion, thinly sliced
- 2 bell peppers, seeded and thinly sliced
- 2 teaspoons olive oil
- 1 teaspoon salt
- 1 garlic clove, chopped
- 1 cup vegan mozzarella shreds

Eggplant Parmesan Pizza

SERVES 4

1 recipe Basic Pizza Dough, uncooked
1 cup Super-Easy Pizza Sauce
1 medium eggplant
½ cup walnuts, ground
¼ cup nutritional yeast
  Pinch of salt
1 teaspoon oil
1 cup nondairy milk
1 cup flour
1 cup bread crumbs
½ teaspoon dried oregano
½ teaspoon dried basil
1 teaspoon salt
2 cups vegan mozzarella shreds
  Olive oil for frying

Deep-fried eggplant parm is a delicious dish that has found its spiritual home on top of a pizza. Load on the cheese and take this hybrid for a spin.

1. Preheat oven to 475°F. Shape dough on a 16-inch pizza pan or on a greased and cornmeal-sprinkled cookie sheet.
2. Spread pizza sauce evenly over dough.
3. Slice eggplant thinly.
4. In a small bowl, mix ground walnuts, nutritional yeast, oil, and a pinch of salt (this will be the Parmesan).
5. In three separate shallow dishes, place milk, flour, and bread crumbs. Add the basil and oregano to the bread crumbs and add salt to the flour.
6. In a large sauté pan, heat about 2 teaspoons olive oil over medium heat.
7. Dip each eggplant into milk, dredge in flour, and dip in milk again, then lastly in bread crumbs.
8. Fry in heated oil for about 3 minutes on each side until golden brown; transfer to paper-lined plate.
9. Once all the eggplant is cooked, place in a spiral pattern on the pizza sauce and top with cheese and "Parmesan."
10. Bake for 20-25 minutes. Slice and enjoy! This pizza keeps really well, so look forward to leftovers for breakfast.

Thai Pizza

Who would think to use peanut sauce in place of pizza sauce? East meets West in this truly unique pie that melds savory, spicy, and fresh flavors with crunchy, creamy, and meaty textures.

1. Preheat oven to 475°F. Shape dough on a 16-inch pizza pan or on a cornmeal-sprinkled cookie sheet.
2. Mix tamarind paste and chili (if using) into Spicy Peanut Sauce. Cut tempeh into 1-inch cubes. In a small bowl, mix tempeh and half of Spicy Peanut Sauce, coating all pieces.
3. Spread the other half of Spicy Peanut Sauce on dough evenly. Top with marinated tempeh and any remaining sauce.
4. Arrange carrot and green onion over tempeh.
5. Bake for 20-25 minutes.
6. Top with peanuts, bean sprouts, and cilantro.

SERVES 4

1 recipe Basic Pizza Dough, uncooked

1 teaspoon tamarind paste

1 red chili pepper, diced (optional)

2 8-ounce packages tempeh

1 recipe Spicy Peanut Sauce (see "Dips for All Seasons")

1 carrot, cut into long, thin strands or grated

2 green onions, cut into long, thin strands

3 tablespoons peanuts, crushed

½ cup bean sprouts

¼ cup cilantro, finely chopped

Black Bean Taco Pizza

SERVES 4

- 1 recipe Basic Pizza Dough, uncooked
- 1 15-ounce can refried black beans
- ½ cup tomato sauce
- 1 tablespoon oil
- 1 8-ounce package tempeh, crumbled
- 1 tablespoon flour
- 1–2 teaspoons chili powder
- 1 teaspoon salt
- 1 teaspoon garlic powder
- 1 teaspoon cumin
- 1 teaspoon minced onion
- 4 cups lettuce greens
- 1 medium tomato, chopped
- 1 ripe avocado, chopped
- ¼ cup cilantro, chopped
- ¼ onion, chopped
- 1 recipe Creamy Southwestern Dip (see "Dips for All Seasons")

Anything with refried beans in it automatically moves to the head of the pack when it comes to junk food. This totally cravable pizza features a mix of pizza sauce and the aforementioned beans—it's like a flat taco!

1. Preheat oven to 475°F. Shape dough on a 16-inch pizza pan or on a greased and cornmeal-sprinkled cookie sheet.
2. Mix black beans and tomato sauce, and spread on pizza dough.
3. In a skillet over medium-high heat, sauté tempeh in oil until golden brown. Stir in flour, chili powder, salt, garlic powder, cumin, and minced onion, and cook until spices become fragrant and tempeh is coated in spice mixture. Add ½ cup water to pan and stir well. Cook for 1 minute.
4. Spread tempeh mixture over black beans.
5. Bake for 20 minutes.
6. Slice with a pizza cutter into 8 or 12 slices.
7. Top each slice with lettuce, tomatoes, avocado, cilantro, onion, and a dollop of Creamy Southwestern Dip.

Pesto Chicken Pizza with Creamy Garlic Sauce

This white pizza flies in the face of conventional pies and comes together in a pinch. Plus, it features Chick'n Strips, a major star in the world of vegan junk food.

1. Preheat oven to 475°F. Shape dough on a 16-inch pizza pan or on a greased and cornmeal-sprinkled cookie sheet.
2. Cut "chicken" strips into thin strips. In a medium bowl, add pesto and chicken strips, stirring to coat chicken pieces. Set aside.
3. In a large skillet over medium heat, sauté garlic in olive oil until it becomes very fragrant, being careful not to let it brown. Add flour to the pan and mix with a whisk, stirring flour into oil. Cook for 1 minute.
4. Slowly add milk and broth, stirring constantly. Stir in beans, nutritional yeast, salt, and pepper, cooking until sauce is creamy and thick. Add more milk a few tablespoons at a time if sauce becomes too thick. Remove from heat.
5. Spread sauce over pizza. Top with chicken strips. Drizzle a few tablespoons of the Basil Pesto over pizza.
6. Bake for 20-25 minutes, slice, and gobble up.

SERVES 4

- 1 recipe Basic Pizza Dough, uncooked
- 1 package vegan chicken strips such as Gardein Chick'n Strips
- 2 tablespoons olive oil
- 3 cloves garlic, chopped
- 4 tablespoons flour
- 1¼ cups nondairy milk
- ½ cup vegetable broth
- 1 15-ounce can white beans, drained and puréed well with vegetable broth
- ½ cup nutritional yeast
- 1 teaspoon salt
- ½ teaspoon pepper
- 1 recipe Basil Pesto (see "Dips for All Seasons")

Deep-Dish Hawaiian Pizza

SERVES 4–6

1 recipe Basic Pizza Dough, uncooked

2 cups Super-Easy Pizza Sauce

1 package vegan deli slices, Tofurky Smoked Hickory, chopped

1 15-ounce can pineapple chunks, drained

2 cups vegan mozzarella shreds

So good and *so* junky! Whoever thought to pair salty meat with pineapple was clearly a genius. This vegan rendition features lots and lots of deli slices, canned fruit, and mozzarella shreds married in a deep, delicious crust.

1. Preheat oven to 475°F. Press dough into bottom and sides of a greased and cornmeal-sprinkled 12-inch springform pan.
2. Pour Super-Easy Pizza Sauce over dough followed by chopped deli slices, pineapple, and mozzarella shreds.
3. Bake for 40–45 minutes or until crust is golden brown and cheese is melted. Let cool for about 10 minutes before cutting. (Good luck eating without a fork!)

Veggie Cheese Baguette Pizza

SERVES 4

2 tablespoons olive oil

2 cups sliced mushrooms

1 medium onion, sliced thinly

2 bell peppers, red or green, sliced thinly

1 clove garlic, minced

1 French bread baguette, cut in half lengthwise

1 cup Super-Easy Pizza Sauce

2 cups vegan mozzarella shreds

Here's a dorm-room favorite revamped with vegan cheese. It's even easier to put together when you have your own kitchen, but still tastes as mouthwateringly good as it did when you were studying for finals.

1. Preheat oven to 400°F. Line a baking sheet with foil.
2. In a skillet, sauté mushrooms, onion, and peppers in olive oil until tender-crisp; add garlic and sauté for 2 more minutes.
3. Place baguette halves on cookie sheet. Spread Super-Easy Pizza Sauce over each, followed by half of the cheese.
4. Divide mushroom mixture between baguette halves. Top with remaining cheese.
5. Bake for 15 minutes or until cheese is melted and bread is crispy.

Rosemary-Garlic Potato Pizza

Truth be told, this is a bit more gourmet than the other junk food offerings in this book. But it's still not something that would be on Weight Watchers' list of approved foods, so I think we're in the clear. This pizza boasts tender potatoes artfully layered over a creamy white garlic sauce with hints of rosemary. Can you say, divine?

1. Preheat oven to 475°F. Shape dough on a 16-inch pizza pan or on a greased and cornmeal-sprinkled cookie sheet.
2. In a 4-quart saucepan over high heat, bring 2 quarts of water to a boil. Place potatoes in water and bring back to a boil. Cook for 5-8 minutes, checking frequently. Potatoes should be al dente, softened but with a bite to them. Drain.
3. In a medium bowl, toss potatoes with olive oil, salt, and rosemary. Rinse and drain white beans. Purée with broth until smooth, set aside.
4. In a large skillet over medium heat, sauté garlic in olive oil until it becomes very fragrant, being careful not to let it brown. Add flour to the pan and mix with a whisk, stirring flour into oil. Cook for 1 minute.
5. Slowly add milk and beans, stirring constantly. Stir in nutritional yeast, salt, and pepper, cooking until sauce is creamy and thick. Add more milk a few tablespoons at a time if sauce gets too thick. Remove from heat.
6. Spread sauce over pizza. Top with potatoes in spiral pattern and drizzle with a small amount of olive oil.
7. Bake for 20-25 minutes. Cool slightly, then cut and share with loved ones.

SERVES 4

- 1 recipe Basic Pizza Dough, uncooked
- 2 medium potatoes, peeled and sliced paper-thin
- 1 tablespoon olive oil
- 1 teaspoon salt
- 2 teaspoons fresh rosemary
- 1 15-ounce can white beans
- ½ cup vegetable broth
- 1 tablespoon olive oil
- 3 cloves garlic, chopped
- 2 tablespoons flour
- 1 cup nondairy milk
- ½ cup nutritional yeast
- 1 teaspoon salt
- ½ teaspoon pepper

Artichoke and Caramelized-Onion Pizza with Balsamic Reduction

SERVES 4

1 recipe of Basic Pizza Dough, uncooked

1 recipe Balsamic Reduction (see "Dips for All Seasons")

3 medium onions, thinly sliced

1 tablespoon olive oil

1 teaspoon salt

1 garlic clove, chopped

1 14-ounce can whole artichoke hearts, drained, quartered

1 cup vegan mozzarella shreds

Sweet caramelized onions, tangy artichokes, rich balsamic on a crisp, light crust. You could pay upwards of $20 at the fancy new wood-fired pizza joint downtown for a similar pie, or you could build it at home for half the cost in less than 1 hour. Your pick.

1. Preheat oven to 475°F. Place rolled or stretched dough on a prepared 16-inch pizza pan or a greased and cornmeal-sprinkled cookie sheet.
2. In a sauté pan over medium-high heat, sauté the onions in olive oil, stirring occasionally, allowing the onions to cook down and turn a deep golden brown. Turn heat down after about 10 minutes and add the salt and garlic. If the onions start to brown too much, lower heat; add a teaspoon of oil if they start to stick. Cook for another 8–10 minutes, stirring occasionally. Remove from heat.
3. Spoon onions onto dough and spread evenly. Top with artichokes and cheese.
4. Bake for 20–25 minutes.
5. Drizzle with Balsamic Reduction and enjoy while piping hot.

Barbecued Tempeh Pizza

Just a few key ingredients make this pizza really special: barbecued marinated tempeh, red onions, and cilantro. It's perfect for dipping into ranch dressing.

1. Preheat oven to 475°F. Shape dough on a 16-inch pizza pan or on a greased and cornmeal-sprinkled cookie sheet.
2. Slice tempeh into ¼-inch slices. Put half the barbecue sauce in a shallow dish and add the sliced tempeh, turning to coat.
3. Spread the other half of the barbecue sauce on crust. Top with tempeh, cheese, and onions.
4. Bake for 20 minutes.
5. Top with cilantro, drizzle with Creamy Ranch Dressing, slice, and devour.

SERVES 4

- 1 recipe Basic Pizza Dough, uncooked
- 2 8-ounce packages tempeh
- 2 cups barbecue sauce
- ½ cup vegan mozzarella shreds
- 1 red onion, sliced thin
- ¼ cup cilantro, finely chopped
- ½ cup Creamy Ranch Dressing (see "Dips for All Seasons")

Pizza Dough Garlic Rolls

SERVES 6

1 recipe Basic Pizza Dough, uncooked
1 cup vegan mozzarella shreds
3 cloves garlic, minced
1 teaspoon salt
½ teaspoon garlic powder
½ teaspoon dried basil
1 tablespoon fresh parsley, chopped
¼ cup nutritional yeast
3 tablespoons olive oil

Sometimes the sauce and toppings just get in the way, right? The melted garlic cheese interior in these bad boys is to die for. You'll want to double the recipe if you have hungry teens to feed.

1. Preheat oven to 350°F. Line a baking sheet with parchment paper.
2. Divide dough into 16-18 pieces. Roll pieces into balls.
3. In a small bowl, mix together cheese and garlic.
4. In each dough ball, press about a tablespoonful of cheese-garlic mixture into the center and close dough around it. Roll back into a smooth ball. Place on prepared baking sheet. Repeat for rest of dough balls.
5. Bake for 20 minutes or until golden brown, shaking baking sheet halfway through cooking to help brown evenly.
6. In a large bowl, mix together salt, garlic powder, basil, parsley, and nutritional yeast.
7. When rolls are hot out of the oven, drizzle with olive oil, turning to coat.
8. Place oiled rolls a few at a time into nutritional yeast mixture, tossing to coat.
9. Serve hot.

Beer Cheese Bread

Thankfully, several brewers make vegan-friendly beers. And despite the fact that it's a beverage, beer is an honorary junk food. With just a few ingredients, you have homemade bread that tastes slightly malty from the brew and super buttery.

1. Preheat oven to 375°F. Lightly grease a 9" × 5" loaf pan.
2. In a medium bowl, mix flour and sugar. Add beer and mix just until dough is combined; do not overmix.
3. Spoon dough into prepared pan.
4. In a small bowl, mix margarine and nutritional yeast and pour over dough.
5. Bake for 40-50 minutes or until a knife comes out clean. Cool on a wire rack.
6. Serve with 1 recipe Green Chili Dip (see "Dips for All Seasons").

For Spicy Beer Cheese Bread, add ¼ cup chopped canned jalapeños to the recipe.

*NOTE: If you do not have self-rising flour, sift together 3 cups all-purpose flour, 4½ teaspoons baking powder, and 1 teaspoon salt.

MAKES 1 LOAF

- 3 cups self-rising flour*
- ¼ cup brown sugar
- 1 12-fluid-ounce beer, light-colored
- ⅓ cup vegan margarine, melted
- ¼ cup nutritional yeast

Drop Biscuits

MAKES A DOZEN

1¾ cup self-rising flour*

¾ cup nondairy milk

3 tablespoons vegan
  mayonnaise

When you need a biscuit quick, look to this easy-peasy recipe. These beauties beg to be drowned in gravy or topped with margarine and jam.

1. Preheat oven to 450°F. Lightly grease a cookie sheet.
2. In medium bowl, combine flour, milk, and mayonnaise until just combined; do not overmix.
3. Drop by the heaping tablespoonful onto prepared baking sheet.
4. Bake for 7-9 minutes or until tops begin to turn golden brown.

*NOTE: If you do not have self-rising flour, sift together 3 cups all-purpose flour, 4½ teaspoons baking powder, and 1 teaspoon salt.

Ranch Garlic Bread

SERVES 6

½ cup vegan margarine,
  softened

2 tablespoons dry Creamy
  Ranch Dressing mix (see
  "Dips for All Seasons")

2 cloves garlic, crushed

1 French bread baguette

At catering events I make this bread all the time and people always want to know the mystery behind it. But there's really nothing to it! It's half herb and half garlic, which makes it a good side to a salad or soup.

1. Preheat oven to 375°F. Line a baking sheet with parchment paper.
2. In a small bowl, mix margarine, Creamy Ranch Dressing mix, and garlic.
3. Slice baguette lengthwise or into 2-inch slices. Divide garlic mixture between two loaves or slices.
4. Place on prepared baking sheet and bake for 10-15 minutes or until bread is toasted and golden. Best enjoyed warm.

Garlic-Onion-Cheese Bread Loaf

This savory loaf benefits from a buttermilk-like flavor that comes when you mix soymilk and apple cider vinegar. Add vegan cheese to the mix for a truly memorable bread that only gets better when toasted and slathered with margarine.

1. Preheat oven to 400°F. Grease a 9" × 5" loaf pan.
2. In a small bowl, mix soymilk and apple cider vinegar; set aside.
3. In a medium sauté pan over medium-high heat, cook the onion and garlic in olive oil, stirring constantly until onions are golden, about 8 minutes. Add pepper. Remove from heat.
4. In a medium bowl, mix flour, baking powder, baking soda, chives, and salt. Stir in soymilk-vinegar mixture, cheese, and onion-garlic mixture, mixing until just combined; do not overmix.
5. Pour mixture into prepared pan. Drizzle with 1 tablespoon olive oil.
6. Bake for 25-30 minutes. Cool completely before cutting.

MAKES 1 LOAF

- ¾ cup soymilk
- 1 teaspoon apple cider vinegar
- 2 teaspoons olive oil
- ½ red onion, chopped
- 3 cloves garlic, chopped
- ½ teaspoon ground pepper
- 2 cups flour
- 2 teaspoons baking powder
- 1 teaspoon baking soda
- 1 teaspoon dried chives
- 1 teaspoon salt
- 1½ cups vegan Cheddar shreds
- 1 tablespoon olive oil

Onion-Garlic Naan

MAKES A DOZEN NAAN

- 1 large onion, finely chopped
- 1 tablespoon olive oil
- 2 cloves garlic, chopped
- ¾ cup lukewarm water
- ⅓ cup vegan margarine, melted
- 1 teaspoon salt
- 3–3¼ cups flour

Most naan you find at the market or out at restaurants are made with buttermilk, an ingredient that's verboten for vegans. It's not a problem here, as I've found a way to create the same light texture while bypassing animal products altogether. Use as a base for a pizza, dip in hummus, or munch on its own. Either way, it satisfies a bread craving.

1. In a medium sauté pan over high heat, cook the onion in the olive oil, stirring occasionally. Add garlic. When the onions are translucent and just golden brown, remove from heat.
2. In a large bowl using a wooden spoon, combine onion-garlic mixture, water, melted margarine, and salt. Begin adding 3 cups of flour ½ cup at a time. Add the extra ¼ cup flour only if you need it to form a smooth dough that doesn't stick to your hands.
3. Form the dough into a large ball and cut into 16 equal pieces; roll each into a ball. On a lightly floured surface, roll each ball into an 8-inch circle.
4. In a large skillet over medium-high heat, place each naan in the pan for about 3-4 minutes on each side.

Tex-Mex Corn Bread

There's corn bread and then there's *corn bread*. Anything but dry, anything but boring, this colorful and spicy twist on the ole Jiffy box mix is the perfect vehicle for melting a generous smear of vegan margarine. Savory eats in this baking dish, I tell ya.

1. Preheat oven to 350°F. Grease a 9" × 9" baking dish.
2. In a large bowl, mix soymilk and apple cider vinegar; set aside to thicken.
3. In a medium bowl, whisk together flour, cornmeal, baking powder, sugar, and salt.
4. To the soymilk-vinegar mixture, add onion, garlic, peppers, shortening, and margarine.
5. Add flour ingredients to the soymilk mixture and stir just to combine; do not overmix.
6. Pour into prepared baking dish.
7. Bake for 40-45 minutes or until a toothpick comes out clean and top is golden brown.

MAKES 6–8 SERVINGS

1½ cups soymilk
1 tablespoon apple cider vinegar
1½ cups flour
1 cup cornmeal
2 teaspoons baking powder
2 tablespoons sugar
1 teaspoon salt
1 small onion, minced
1 clove garlic, minced
1 jalapeño pepper, seeded and chopped
1 red bell pepper, seeded and finely chopped
¼ cup vegan nonhydrogenated shortening, softened
2 tablespoons vegan margarine, softened

CHAPTER 5

Festive Grub

Vegan Party Essentials

Oven-Roasted Corn with Cheesy Chile Lime Butter

SERVES 6

6 ears of corn, shucked

6 tablespoons vegan margarine, melted

Juice of 3 limes

2 teaspoons salt

½ teaspoon cayenne pepper

¼ cup nutritional yeast

These ears give regular old corn on the cob a serious run for its money. The hardest part of this recipe is shucking the corn, so why not bring this to your next barbecue? You're sure to make a boatload of new friends—and quite possibly some new fans.

If making in the oven:

1. Preheat oven to 400°F.
2. In a large baking dish, place corn, margarine, lime juice, salt, cayenne pepper, and nutritional yeast. Roll corn around in mixture. Cover tightly with foil.
3. Bake for 35 minutes.

If making on the grill:

1. Peel back the husk and remove silk; replace husk and grill for about 30 minutes or until tender.
2. To serve, remove husk and place corn on a serving platter; brush each with melted margarine.
3. In a small bowl, whisk together lime juice, salt, cayenne, and nutritional yeast. Pour over corn, turning to coat. Serve immediately.

Baked Onion Dip

Remember the onion dip you make from dried onion soup and sour cream, the one that you'd pair with potato chips and devour in one sitting? This one's better.

1. Preheat oven to 350°F. Have ready a 1-quart baking dish.
2. In a medium sauté pan over medium-high heat, sauté onions, garlic, and salt in oil until caramelized, about 15 minutes.
3. In a medium bowl, cream mayonnaise and cream cheese, then add parsley and half of mozzarella cheese. Add onion mixture and stir to combine.
4. Spoon into baking dish. Top with remaining mozzarella cheese.
5. Bake for 30 minutes or until bubbly and cheese is melted. Serve with bread or crackers.

SERVES 4–6

- 1 large sweet onion, cut in half and sliced thin
- 1 clove garlic, minced
- 1 teaspoon salt
- 1 tablespoon olive oil
- ½ cup vegan mayonnaise
- 1 8-ounce container vegan cream cheese, softened
- 1 tablespoon dried parsley
- 1 cup vegan mozzarella shreds
  Sliced baguette or crackers

Stuffed Mushrooms

SERVES 6

1 pound baby bella mushrooms

¼ cup chopped onions

1 clove garlic, minced

2 tablespoons vegan margarine

½ cup vegan cream cheese

¾ cup bread crumbs

½ teaspoon oregano

½ teaspoon salt

½ teaspoon pepper

½ cup bread crumbs

Truly a contrast in textures, this gives your mouth a pleasant surprise with each bite. Baby bellas add a depth of flavor and hold up nicely to baking, but button mushrooms are readily available and work nicely too. Your choice!

1. Preheat oven to 375°F. Line a baking sheet with parchment paper.
2. Remove and finely chop mushroom stems.
3. In a medium sauté pan over medium-high heat, sauté mushroom pieces, onions, and garlic in margarine until onions are translucent.
4. In a medium bowl, beat cream cheese with a whisk until creamy, then stir in cooked mushroom mixture, bread crumbs, oregano, salt, and pepper.
5. Spoon a heaping teaspoonful of cream cheese mixture into each mushroom cap. Dip cream cheese in bread crumbs and place on prepared baking sheet.
6. Bake for 8-10 minutes. These can be served hot or at room temperature if you plan to take them to a party.

Falafel with Tahini Dip

As far as I'm concerned, falafel should be a food group unto itself. And even though it's deep-fried, it feels healthy, so I consider it a no-guilt junk food. It's super cheap to buy bulk dry garbanzo beans, so this is a good option for the budget-conscious.

SERVES 4

1 cup dried chickpeas (garbanzo beans)
2 tablespoons onion, minced
1 clove garlic, minced
1 teaspoon cumin
1 teaspoon baking powder
2 tablespoons parsley, finely chopped
¼ cup water
Oil for frying

1. Soak chickpeas overnight or for at least 6 hours.
2. When ready to cook, in a deep frying pan over medium-high heat, bring about 2 inches of oil to 350°F. On a baking sheet, place crumpled paper towels to drain falafel as they cook.
3. Drain chickpeas and place in a food processor; process until beans are very finely ground.
4. Add onion, garlic, cumin, baking powder, and parsley. Process adding water a tablespoon at a time until mixture holds together when a spoonful is pressed in your hand.
5. Shape heaping tablespoonfuls of chickpea mix into slightly flattened disks.
6. Cook in preheated oil for 3-5 minutes or until golden on both sides. Remove to prepared baking sheet.
7. Serve with Tahini Dip.

Tahini Dip

1. In a small bowl, whisk together tahini and water until smooth.
2. Add lemon juice, salt, and garlic.
3. Keep in an airtight container and use within 3 days.

½ cup tahini
¼ cup water
2 tablespoons fresh lemon juice
½ teaspoon salt
1 clove garlic, crushed

Beer Tempura Vegetables

SERVES 4

1 12-ounce vegan beer, very cold

2 cups flour

2 teaspoons baking powder

½ cup cornstarch

1 recipe Wasabi Soy Dipping Sauce (see "Dips for All Seasons")

Vegetables: broccoli florets, cauliflower florets, red pepper slices, yams (thinly sliced lengthwise), green beans, onion slices, button mushrooms, carrot sticks, or zucchini slices

Best served hot, these light, crisp veggies have just a hint of beer flavor. Bring them to a party and you're sure to be invited back time and time again.

1. In a deep-sided pan over medium-high heat, bring about 3 inches of oil to 350°F. Line a baking sheet with crumpled paper towels to drain cooked vegetables on.
2. In a medium bowl, mix together cold beer, flour, and baking powder until smooth.
3. Dredge vegetables in cornstarch. Dip in batter, allowing excess to drip off.
4. Fry in heated oil for 5-7 minutes or until golden brown. Drain on prepared baking sheet.
5. Transfer to a serving plate and set out a small bowl of Wasabi Soy Dipping Sauce for dipping.

Foil-Wrapped Tempeh

It might seem strange to fry these while they're wrapped in foil, but trust me, it works to seal in the moisture in the marinated tempeh. If you don't have five-spice powder, you can make your own by combining Szechuan peppercorns and star anise (toasted and put through a spice grinder), with ground cloves, ground cinnamon, and ground fennel seeds.

1. Cut tempeh lengthwise and then into triangular-shaped pieces.
2. In a medium bowl, mix soy sauce, sherry, ginger, brown sugar, five-spice powder, olive oil, and sesame oil. Gently toss tempeh in marinade, coating all sides. Marinate in the refrigerator overnight.
3. Wrap each tempeh triangle tightly in foil, folding a piece over and then folding edges of foil down tightly toward tempeh.
4. In a large sauté pan over medium-high heat, bring 2 inches of oil to 350°F. Fry packets for 2 minutes, remove from oil with a slotted spoon, and drain on crumpled paper towels.
5. Serve when packets are cool enough to be handled.

SERVES 4

- 1 8-ounce package tempeh
- 2 tablespoons light soy sauce
- 1 tablespoon dry sherry
- 2 teaspoons ginger, grated
- 1 teaspoon brown sugar
- 1 teaspoon five-spice powder
- 1 tablespoon olive oil
- ½ teaspoon sesame oil
- Oil for frying

Sausage Puffs

SERVES 6

½ onion, chopped

1 package vegan Gimme Lean Sausage

1 tablespoon oil

1 tablespoon dried parsley

1 cup bread crumbs

¼ cup vegan mayonnaise

1 11-ounce package puff pastry sheets (Pepperidge Farm brand is vegan)

This really is the ultimate junk food. Not only do you have super-salty sausage mixed with onion, mayo, and bread crumbs, but you fold it all in a decadent, flaky puff pastry. Expect to be asked for this recipe if you serve it at brunch.

1. Preheat oven to 350°F. Line a baking sheet with parchment paper.
2. In a medium sauté pan over medium-high heat, cook onion and sausage in oil, breaking sausage up into small pieces. Cook until sausage and onion are lightly browned. Remove from heat, transfer to a bowl, and cool completely before next step.
3. Add parsley and bread crumbs. Stir in mayonnaise.
4. On a large cutting board using a sharp knife, cut pastry lengthwise so that you have two long rectangles of dough. Place dough on prepared baking sheet.
5. Place half of sausage mixture in a long row down the middle of each dough rectangle.
6. Fold dough over sausage, making a long skinny rectangle. Crimp open edges closed with a fork. Cut into 2-inch-wide slices. Separate lightly on a cookie sheet.
7. Bake for 15-20 minutes or until very golden brown.

Sun-Dried Tomato and Turkey Pinwheels

Don't let the spinach in this recipe fool you; these are more delicious than they are healthy. Plus, they whip up in a matter of minutes and you can easily double or triple the recipe if you're expecting a hoard of friends at your house!

1. In a small bowl, mix cream cheese and sun-dried tomatoes until smooth.
2. On each tortilla, spread a heaping tablespoonful of cream cheese mixture evenly with a rubber spatula. Arrange spinach on top of cream cheese, followed by deli slices.
3. Roll into a tight cylinder. Cut each into 1½-inch wheels. Refrigerate until ready to eat.

SERVES 4

- 1 8-ounce container cream cheese
- 1 3-ounce jar oil-packed sun-dried tomatoes, chopped
- 6 tortillas
- 2 cups baby spinach
- 2 5-ounce packages vegan turkey deli slices

Teriyaki Pineapple Tempeh Kabobs

SERVES 4

1 recipe Pineapple Teriyaki
Sauce (see "Dips for All
Seasons")

1 8-ounce package tempeh,
cubed

2 cups pineapple, cubed

2 cups cherry tomatoes

1 small red onion, cut into
large chunks

2 tablespoons olive oil

Wooden skewers, soaked in
water for 15 minutes.

Aside from the straight salty or straight saccharine, most junk food
shares the common bond of having a savory *and* sweet flavor profile.
On display here is a terrific example, inspired by the islands.

1. Preheat oven to 400°F. Line a baking sheet with parchment paper. Or
   heat your barbecue if grilling.
2. In a medium bowl, toss Pineapple Teriyaki Sauce and tempeh, then
   marinate for 2 hours.
3. On each skewer, alternate tempeh, pineapple, cherry tomatoes, and
   onions. Place on prepared baking sheet.
4. Brush vegetables with Pineapple Teriyaki Sauce and olive oil.
5. Bake for 20 minutes or until onions are tender.

To grill:
1. Brush grate with oil and grill for 10-12 minutes, turning once halfway
   through cooking.

Buffalo Tempeh Dip

With this I present a creamy, cheesy, hot sauce-infused dip with tempeh chunks, best enjoyed piping hot with celery sticks or a hunk of crusty French bread.

1. Preheat oven to 350°F. Lightly grease a 9" × 13" baking dish.
2. In baking dish, mix tempeh cubes with hot sauce.
3. In a small bowl, mix cream cheese and Creamy Ranch Dressing with celery and pour over tempeh mixture.
4. Cover tightly with foil.
5. Bake for 20 minutes, remove foil, and top with shreds.
6. Bake for an additional 15-20 minutes or until shreds are melted.
7. Serve with celery sticks and French bread torn into chunks.

SERVES 6

- 2 8-ounce packages of tempeh, cubed
- 1 12-ounce bottle Frank's RedHot Sauce
- 2 8-ounce containers vegan cream cheese
- 1 recipe Creamy Ranch Dressing (see "Dips for All Seasons")
- ¾ cup celery, chopped
- 1 cup vegan mozzarella shreds
- 6 ribs celery, cut into large sticks
- 1 French bread baguette

Taquitos with Avocado Sauce

SERVES 4

2 large potatoes, peeled and chopped

1 teaspoon salt

1 12-ounce package Soyrizo, vegan Mexican sausage (about 1 cup)

1 tablespoon oil

1 teaspoon cumin

8 corn tortillas

Oil for frying

1 recipe Avocado Sauce (see "Dips for All Seasons")

Fry it and you're well on the way to making it an irresistible junk food. In this case, you've also got some mighty tasty flavors melding, so you've got to give credit where credit's due.

1. Line a baking sheet with crumpled paper towels for draining cooked taquitos.
2. In a medium saucepan, bring enough salted water to boil to cover potatoes.
3. Cook until fork-tender. Remove from heat and drain.
4. In a medium sauté pan over medium-high heat, cook Soyrizo, stirring frequently for 4 minutes. Add cumin and potatoes to the pan and mash with a fork until mixture is mostly smooth and combined. Remove from heat.
5. On a dry sauté pan over medium heat, heat corn tortillas on each side just until soft. Keep warm wrapped in a clean kitchen towel.
6. Preheat a large frying pan over medium-high heat; add about 3 tablespoons oil to pan.
7. For each taquito, spoon a heaping tablespoon of potato mixture and spread evenly. Roll and secure with a toothpick.
8. Fry in heated oil (toothpick and all) for about 2 minutes on each side or until evenly golden brown. Place on prepared baking sheet.
9. Serve with Avocado Sauce.

Beer-Barbecued Meatballs

Let someone else serve Swedish meatballs; I'd rather put out these happy little vegan balls cooked in a beer-infused barbecue marinade. The best part? Gobbling them up with toothpicks. You can use pre-made vegan meatballs in a pinch, but here's how to do it from scratch.

1. Preheat oven to 350°F. Line a baking sheet with parchment paper.
2. In a small saucepan, bring broth to a boil and add textured vegetable protein. Turn heat off and allow TVP to reconstitute 10 minutes. Drain very well, squeezing liquid out.
3. In a small bowl, mix flaxseeds with water; set aside.
4. In a medium sauté pan, cook onions in oil, stirring until translucent; add garlic, sauté for 1 more minute. Remove from heat.
5. In a large bowl, combine all the ingredients except the beer and barbecue sauce and mix with hands until very well combined. If the mixture is too dry to be shaped into a ball, add 1 more tablespoon of tomato paste. If mixture is too wet, add ¼ cup bread crumbs at a time until you can easily shape into 1½-inch balls.
6. Place balls on prepared baking sheet.
7. Bake for 25-30 minutes, carefully turning meatballs halfway through cooking. Meatballs are done when deep golden brown.
8. In a large saucepan, mix beer and barbecue sauce, add meatballs, and bring to a boil. Turn heat down to medium-low and let simmer for 15-20 minutes.
9. Serve on a serving platter with toothpicks and extra sauce in a small bowl.

SERVES 6

2 cups vegan beef broth
1 cup textured vegetable protein granules
2 tablespoons ground flaxseeds
¼ cup water
½ onion, diced
1 teaspoon olive oil
1 clove garlic, chopped
1 tablespoon tomato paste
1 teaspoon vegan Worcestershire sauce
1 teaspoon light soy sauce
½ cup bread crumbs
½ cup walnuts, finely minced
½ teaspoon oregano
½ teaspoon parsley
½ teaspoon basil
1 12-ounce beer
2 cups barbecue sauce

Pizza Rolls

SERVES 4

1½ cups Super-Easy Pizza Sauce (see "Crusts and Carbs")
1 cup vegan pepperoni, finely chopped
1 cup vegan mozzarella shreds
1 package vegan won ton wrappers
Oil for frying

Pizza toppings, deep-fried in a won ton wrapper equals junk food bliss.

1. In a frying pan, heat about 2 inches of oil to 360°F. Line a baking sheet with crumpled paper towels to drain cooked pizza rolls.
2. In a medium bowl, mix Super-Easy Pizza Sauce, pepperoni, and cheese.
3. Brush edges of won ton wrapper with water; place a scant teaspoon of pizza sauce mixture on won ton and fold over, pressing edge to seal completely.
4. Fry pizza rolls on each side for 2-3 minutes or until golden brown. Place on prepared baking sheet.

Green Chili Quesadilla

SERVES 4

1 15-ounce cans cannellini beans, rinsed and drained
1½ cups vegan mozzarella shreds
1 4-ounce can diced green chilies
1 teaspoon salt
1 teaspoon cumin
4–6 tortillas
1 teaspoon oil
1 recipe Creamy Southwestern Dip (see "Dips for All Seasons")

Yo quiero Taco Bell? Well, the ingredients in this quesadilla—white beans, green chilies, and cheese shreds—are vegan but combine perfectly to make a melty and mouthwatering Mexican dish.

1. In a small bowl, mash beans with a potato masher until mostly smooth; stir in cheese, chilies, salt, and cumin.
2. Spoon a heaping tablespoonful of this spread on ½ of a tortilla and fold over. Continue for the rest of tortillas.
3. In a large sauté pan over medium-high heat, heat a thin layer of oil and cook quesadillas until lightly browned and crisp. Cut into triangles and serve with Creamy Southwestern Dip.

Ham-Wrapped Asparagus with Chive Cream Cheese

How do you turn asparagus into junk food? Wrap it in cream cheese and ham, that's how.

1. Bring a quart of salted water to boil in a pan that will accommodate asparagus spears.
2. Snap off woody ends of asparagus. Add asparagus to boiling water. Cook for 3-5 minutes or until cooked through but not mushy. Remove from heat and drain; run cold water over asparagus to stop them from overcooking. Set aside to cool.
3. In a small bowl, combine cream cheese, mustard, chives, and salt.
4. On each deli slice, spread a heaping teaspoonful of cream cheese mixture evenly.
5. Roll deli slice around a spear of asparagus. Set on a serving platter and repeat for rest of spears. Refrigerate until ready to serve.

SERVES 4

- 1 bunch asparagus spears (10–12 spears)
- 1 8-ounce package vegan cream cheese
- 1 teaspoon Dijon mustard
- 1 tablespoon fresh chives, minced
- ½ teaspoon salt
- 1 5-ounce package vegan deli slices

Loaded Nachos

SERVES 4

2 teaspoons vegan beef bouillon paste

2 cups water

½ cup small-grain textured vegetable protein (Bob's Red Mill)

½ onion, chopped

1 tablespoon oil

1 teaspoon chili powder

1 teaspoon cumin

½ teaspoon pepper

½ teaspoon garlic powder

1 15-ounce can refried pinto beans

¼ cup nondairy milk

Tortilla chips

1 jalapeño, seeded and sliced

1 cup vegan Cheddar shreds

3 green onions, white and green parts, sliced thinly

¼ cup chopped cilantro

1 cup guacamole

1 cup Vegan Sour Cream (see "Dips for All Seasons")

1 medium tomato, seeded and diced

A staple for your next vegan Super Bowl gathering, or any time you have a hankering for a heap of tortilla chips smothered in spicy-beefy TVP, refried beans, and jalapeño; baked until the cheese gets all melty; and topped with a generous dollop of tomatoes, guac, and sour cream. Classic.

1. In a small saucepan, bring water and bouillon paste to a boil, then stir in TVP. Place a lid on the pot and remove from heat. Let sit 10 minutes. Drain well. Place TVP into a clean kitchen towel and squeeze to completely remove excess liquid.
2. Preheat oven to 375°F. Have a large ovenproof platter or a 9" × 13" baking dish ready.
3. In a medium sauté pan over medium heat, sauté TVP and onion in oil until TVP is browned and onion is translucent and soft, 8–10 minutes. Add chili powder, cumin, pepper, and garlic powder, stirring until mixed well and fragrant. Remove from heat.
4. In a small saucepan, heat refried beans with milk, stirring until heated through. Remove from heat.
5. Place tortilla chips on prepared baking dish in an even double layer.
6. Spoon beans over chips, followed by TVP mixture, cheese, and jalapeños.
7. Bake for 8–10 minutes or until cheese is melted.
8. Top nachos with green onion, cilantro, guacamole, Vegan Sour Cream, and diced tomatoes.

Zucchini Pancakes

Know how to turn the glut of zucchini from your garden into bonafide junk food? Turn them into pancakes and deep-fry those suckers! A real crowd favorite.

1. Grate zucchini, toss with salt, and place in a colander to drain for about 20 minutes.
2. In a frying pan, heat about 1 inch of oil over medium-high heat to about 360°F. Line a baking sheet with crumbled paper towels to drain cooked pancakes on.
3. In a small bowl, combine flaxseeds with water. Set aside.
4. Place zucchini and onion in a kitchen towel and squeeze excess moisture out.
5. In a medium bowl, mix zucchini, onion, flaxseed mixture, cornmeal, flour, and pepper.
6. Place a heaping tablespoon of zucchini mixture into prepared oil, flattening slightly with a spatula.
7. Fry for 3-4 minutes on each side or until golden brown. Remove and place on prepared baking sheet.
8. Serve while still warm with a side dish of Vegan Sour Cream.

SERVES 4

2 medium-sized zucchinis
1 teaspoon salt
1 teaspoon flaxseeds, ground
1 tablespoon water
4 tablespoons onion, grated
¼ cup cornmeal
¼ cup flour
½ teaspoon pepper
  Oil for frying
1 cup Vegan Sour Cream (see "Dips for All Seasons")

Jalapeño Bacon Poppers

SERVES 4–6

Oil for frying
1 8-ounce container vegan cream cheese
1½ cups vegan Cheddar shreds
2 teaspoons vegan bacon bits
10 jalapeño peppers
½ cup cornstarch
1 cup nondairy milk
½ cup flour
1 cup fine bread crumbs
1 teaspoon salt

Nonvegans would look at this recipe title and think, "Bacon? What's up with that?" Fortunately, several manufacturers have specialized in veganizing our junk food favorites, namely cheese and meat stuffs, so we, too, can enjoy crispy fried poppers with a molten creamy bacony filling.

1. In a frying pan, heat about 2-3 inches of oil over medium-high heat; oil should be between 350°F and 375°F. Line a baking sheet with crumbled paper towels to drain cooked poppers on.
2. In a small bowl, mix cream cheese, cheese, and bacon bits.
3. Using gloves to protect fingers from chili, slice jalapeños lengthwise and discard seeds and veins.
4. In three separate shallow bowls, place cornstarch, milk, and flour mixed with bread crumbs and salt.
5. Spoon a heaping teaspoonful of cream cheese mixture into each jalapeño half.
6. Dredge poppers in cornstarch, milk, then bread-crumb mixture. Lay them on a sheet of parchment paper. Redredge in milk and bread crumbs.
7. Fry poppers in batches in prepared oil for 3-5 minutes or until golden. Set poppers on prepared baking sheet to drain.
8. Transfer to a serving platter and serve while still piping hot. Yum!

Corn Dogs page 64

Blueberry Streusel Muffins page 11

Red Velvet Whoopie Pies page 181

Chicken Potpie page 50

Chicken Salad with Walnuts, Apples, and Celery page 37

Veggie Cheese Baguette Pizza page 86

Meatball Pizza with Peppers and Onions page 81

Loaded Nachos
page 112

Spinach Artichoke
Dip page 130

Caramel Popcorn
page 142

Chocolate Chunk Brownies page 211

Baked Curried Sweet Potato Fries page 138

White Chocolate Raspberry Cheesecake page 152

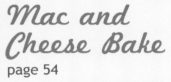

Mac and Cheese Bake
page 54

Meatball Subwich page 36

Barbecue Chip–Crusted Tofu Bites

Ready for the crunchiest tofu you've ever had? Blame potato chips and deep-frying for the delicious result.

1. In a large, deep pan, heat about 3 inches of oil to 345°F.
2. Cut tofu into 1-inch cubes.
3. Place cornstarch in a plastic bag large enough to hold tofu.
4. In a medium bowl, combine flour, baking powder, and ice water. Stir to make a thick batter; do not overmix. A few lumps are okay.
5. Pour barbecue chips into a shallow dish.
6. Place tofu into bag with cornstarch and shake to evenly coat tofu cubes.
7. A few at a time, dip tofu cubes into batter, letting excess drip off, then roll in barbecue chip crumbs.
8. Carefully place tofu into heated oil and fry for about 2 minutes. Remove to paper towels to drain.
9. Transfer to a groovy serving platter and put out a side of Creamy Ranch Dressing to encourage dipping.

SERVES 4–6

Oil for frying
1 16-ounce container extra-firm tofu, drained, frozen, and then thawed
½ cup cornstarch
¾ cup flour
½ teaspoon baking powder
1 cup ice water
1 cup barbecue potato chips, crushed
1 recipe Creamy Ranch Dressing (see "Dips for All Seasons")

Tofu Satay with Soy Wasabi Dipping Sauce

SERVES 4

- 1 tablespoon lemongrass, finely chopped
- 1 tablespoon ginger, grated
- 1 clove garlic, crushed
- 1 tablespoon agave
- 1 tablespoon chili sauce or 1 red chili seeded and thinly sliced (optional)
- ½ teaspoon sesame oil
- 3 tablespoons light soy sauce
- 1 12-ounce package extra-firm tofu, drained, frozen, thawed, and cut into even bite-size squares.
- 1 recipe Wasabi Soy Dipping Sauce (see "Dips for All Seasons")
- Wooden skewers soaked in water for 15 minutes before cooking

Aside from being packed with protein, tofu takes on the flavor of just about anything, making it an almost magical food and a vegan staple. In this recipe, the longer you're able to marinade the tofu, the more flavor you'll pack into your satay.

1. In a shallow dish, combine lemongrass, ginger, garlic, agave, chili sauce (if using), sesame oil, and soy sauce. Add tofu chunks, turning to coat, in marinade. Refrigerate for a few hours or overnight, stirring to make sure all the tofu stays coated in the marinade.
2. Preheat oven to 300°F. If barbecuing, heat your grill. Place 4 or 5 pieces of tofu on each skewer, place on a cookie sheet, and brush with olive oil.
3. Bake for 40 minutes, turning each skewer every 15 minutes.

To cook on the grill:
1. Brush the grate with oil and cook for 10-12 minutes, turning once halfway through cooking.
2. Serve with a generous side of Wasabi Soy Dipping Sauce for dipping.

Corn Fritters

We've taken a detour to the Deep South with this deep-fried treasure. Double the deliciousness if you've got a crowd to feed. For a real down-home feast, serve with a side of vegan ribs, crunchy slaw, and a pitcher of spiked lemonade.

1. Place milk and apple cider vinegar in a small bowl and set aside for 5 minutes.
2. In a medium bowl, combine flour, baking powder, salt, baking soda, and paprika.
3. Add 1 tablespoon oil to the milk mixture. Stir wet ingredients into dry ingredients until just combined, then add corn.
4. Heat about 1 inch of oil in a pan and drop fritters by the heaping tablespoonful. Fry on each side until golden.
5. Drain on paper towels before setting out to serve. Add a generous smear of vegan margarine for the yummiest results.

SERVES 4–6

½ cup soymilk
1 teaspoon apple cider vinegar
¾ cup flour
1 teaspoon baking powder
¼ teaspoon salt
¼ teaspoon baking soda
⅛ teaspoon paprika
1 tablespoon oil
1 cup frozen corn kernels, thawed, drained
Oil for frying

Eggplant Caviar

SERVES 4

1 large eggplant
2 cloves garlic
¾ cup Vegan Sour Cream
(see "Dips for All Seasons")
1 tablespoon fresh lemon
juice
1 teaspoon salt
½ teaspoon pepper

It feels particularly festive to tell someone, "Oh, I'll bring a side of Eggplant Caviar!" even though this recipe technically has very little in common with actual caviar (which is fish roe). No matter! Junk food is all about the fun factor, so I'm sticking to it.

1. Preheat oven to 350°F. Cut eggplant in half lengthwise, place cut side down on parchment-lined cookie sheet, and place a clove of garlic under each side. Bake for 40 minutes or until very soft. When cool enough to handle, spoon eggplant out of skin and roughly chop with garlic.
2. In a medium bowl, mix sour cream, lemon juice, salt, and pepper. Stir in eggplant.
3. Serve with pita chips and be sure to refrigerate leftovers.

CHAPTER 6

Dips for All Seasons

...and All Reasons

Vegan Ricotta

MAKES 2 CUPS

- 8 ounces firm tofu, crumbled into tiny pieces
- 1 8-ounce container vegan cream cheese, softened
- 1 tablespoon lemon juice
- 2 tablespoons nutritional yeast
- 1 teaspoon dried parsley
- 1 teaspoon salt

Look here when you want to make such staples as lasagna or stuffed shells. (And see if you can fool your Italian grandma!)

1. In a medium bowl, stir together tofu and cream cheese with a whisk until well combined.
2. Add lemon juice, nutritional yeast, parsley, and salt. Refrigerate overnight for best results.

Vegan Sour Cream

MAKES ABOUT 2 CUPS

- 1 16-ounce package of silken tofu
- 4 tablespoons oil
- 4 tablespoons lemon juice
- 1 teaspoon salt

This is so easy to whip up, there's no need to go the store-bought route: a vegan staple that is tangy, cool, and creamy.

1. Mix tofu, oil, lemon juice, and salt in a food processor or blender until very smooth. Taste for correct tartness and add more lemon juice if necessary.
2. Be sure to store in the fridge when not using.

Cheese Sauce

It's vegan Velveeta! In this clever fake-out, the vegetables provide body and color and the result is a thick, rich sauce with lots of mild cheese flavor. Generously pour this sauce over pasta, potatoes, broccoli, or nachos.

1. In a saucepan over high heat, bring the potato, carrots, cauliflower, and broth to a boil, then cover and turn the heat down to low. Cook until vegetables are very soft, about 10-12 minutes. Drain.
2. Place vegetables in a food processor and process until they become smooth. Add nutritional yeast, cream cheese, mustard, turmeric, and onion powder.
3. Pour mixture into a large saucepan over medium-high heat.
4. In a small bowl, blend margarine and flour together to make a paste. When saucepan comes to a boil, whisk in the margarine-flour mixture. Whisk in milk and allow mixture to cook until to desired thickness. Remove from heat.

MAKES ABOUT 4 CUPS

1 potato, peeled and chopped into 2-inch pieces

4 carrots, chopped into 2-inch pieces

¼ head of cauliflower, chopped into 2-inch pieces

2 cups vegetable broth

1 cup nutritional yeast

1 8-ounce container vegan cream cheese

1 teaspoon Dijon mustard

1 teaspoon turmeric

1 teaspoon onion powder

¼ cup vegan margarine

¼ cup flour

2 cups nondairy milk

Balsamic Reduction

MAKES ABOUT 1 CUP

1 bottle balsamic vinegar
(about 12 ounces)
¼ cup brown sugar

Here's a staple you don't know you're missing until you have it on hand to drizzle over pizza or a salad. Sweet and slightly tart, Balsamic Reduction wakes up everything it touches, from sandwiches to roasted vegetables, ice cream, and beyond.

1. In a medium saucepan over medium-high heat, bring the balsamic to a boil and stir in sugar.
2. Reduce heat to medium; cook for 15-20 minutes. Note where the balsamic reaches the side of the pan; you want it to reduce down until you have 25 percent of what you started with.
3. When it's done, the reduction will be thick enough to coat the back of a spoon.

Avocado Sauce

MAKES ABOUT 1½ CUPS

2 avocados
1 jalapeño or 1 serrano pepper, depending on heat desired, seeded
1 tablespoon fresh lime juice
1 teaspoon salt
A few sprigs cilantro
⅛ onion, chopped finely
About ½–1 cup water

Because it's so much thinner than guacamole, sometimes I think this recipe wants to be a chilled soup, and I would eat it that way in a heartbeat. But for the purposes of this book—and because the buttery flavor of avocado takes a back seat to the bite of jalapeño and fresh notes of lime and cilantro—consider how to incorporate this street taco condiment into your Mexican-inspired dishes.

1. In a blender, blend all ingredients using water about a ¼ cup at a time to make a somewhat-thin sauce.
2. Keeps in the refrigerator for 2 days.

Pineapple Teriyaki Sauce

A sweet, salty, thick marinade that makes anything it comes in contact with a special treat.

1. In a small bowl, whisk the cornstarch into the soy sauce.
2. Add all ingredients to a medium saucepan and bring to a boil. Simmer until sauce thickens, about 10-15 minutes.

MAKES 2 CUPS

- 1 cup soy sauce
- 3 tablespoons cornstarch
- 1 20-ounce can chunk pineapple (packed in 100 percent pineapple juice)
- ½ cup packed brown sugar
- 1 teaspoon garlic, peeled and chopped

Spicy Peanut Sauce

Addicted to the peanut sauce at the Thai place down the street? Now you can recreate it in the comfort of your own home—and slather it on anything you please!

1. In a large bowl, combine all of the ingredients using a whisk, tasting for a balance of hot and sweet.
2. Refrigerate in an airtight container and use within 4 days.

MAKES 1½ CUPS

- ¾ cup peanut butter, creamy or chunky
- ¼ cup lime juice
- 1 jalapeño, seeded for less heat, minced
- ½ cup seasoned rice vinegar
- ¼ cup brown sugar
- 2 tablespoons cilantro, finely chopped
- ½ teaspoon salt

Wasabi Soy Dipping Sauce

MAKES ABOUT 1 CUP

½ cup soy sauce, low-sodium

¼ cup seasoned rice vinegar

2 teaspoons wasabi paste

Try to get your hands on low-sodium soy sauce for this recipe; otherwise, the sauce can become overpowered by the saltiness. Want to ratchet the heat? Increase the amount of wasabi paste (but be sure to keep your dining guests in mind before you go too crazy)!

1. Whisk together soy sauce and vinegar. Add wasabi 1 teaspoon at a time to desired heat. A great dipping sauce for egg rolls and won tons, or mixed into rice.
2. Keep leftover sauce in the refrigerator and use within 2 days.

Basil Pesto

MAKES ABOUT 1 CUP

⅓ cup pine nuts

2 cups fresh basil

2 cloves garlic

¼ cup nutritional yeast

1 teaspoon salt

½ cup extra-virgin olive oil

Pesto, presto! Whip up a batch of this versatile condiment with all sorts of variations. It's delicious when simply slathered on a slice of fresh, crusty bread.

1. In a food processor, add the nuts and basil; process until basil is finely chopped. Add garlic, nutritional yeast, and salt. Drizzle in olive oil while machine is running.
2. Refrigerate leftovers in an airtight container and use within 5 days.

Sun-Dried Tomato Pesto
1. Add a 3-ounce bag of whole sun-dried tomatoes to the food processor with the basil.

Cilantro Pesto
1. Add 2 cups fresh cilantro instead of the basil, and add walnuts instead of pine nuts. Take out the nutritional yeast and add in about a teaspoon of finely chopped jalapeño.

Easy Salsa Fresca

Quick-to-put-together salsa but with all the flavor of a great salsa, this pairs well with tofu scramble or tortilla chips when a snack attack hits.

1. Mix all ingredients and refrigerate for a few hours to develop flavors.
2. Use within 4 days.

2 medium tomatoes, seeded and chopped

1 jalapeño pepper, seeded and chopped

¼ cup chopped onion

¼ cup cilantro, finely chopped

Juice of 1 lime

1 teaspoon salt

Creamy Southwestern Dip

Need a dip for tortilla chips or to dollop on top of your vegan chili? Look no further: This creamy salsa fresca will do the trick.

1. In a medium bowl, combine all ingredients. Whisk the mixture until smooth. Refrigerate for at least 1 hour so that the dip firms up a bit before serving.
2. Store leftovers in an airtight container and use within 4 days.

MAKES 2 CUPS

1 medium tomato, seeded and diced small

¼ cup finely chopped cilantro

1 jalapeño, seeded, finely minced

⅛ onion, finely minced

1 teaspoon dried parsley

½ teaspoon salt

¼ teaspoon ground cumin

1 cup Vegan Sour Cream (see recipe in this chapter)

½ cup vegan mayonnaise

Creamy Ranch Dressing

MAKES 1 CUP

- ½ cup saltine crackers, ground fine
- ½ cup dried parsley
- 1 tablespoon dried minced onion
- 1 teaspoon dried chives
- 1 tablespoon garlic powder
- 1 teaspoon onion powder
- 2 teaspoons salt
- 1 teaspoon pepper
- ½ cup vegan mayonnaise
- ½ cup Vegan Sour Cream (see recipe in this chapter)
- ¼ cup soymilk

Oniony, creamy, and rich. Prep the dry ingredients and keep the mixture on hand for whenever you need to pull together a dressing in a jiffy. I find that this adds a bit of life to almost all foods—it can definitely turn some foods junky!

1. Mix all the dry ingredients (Creamy Ranch Dressing mix) and store in plastic container. Makes about 1 cup.
2. To make dip, mix 1 tablespoon Creamy Ranch Dressing mix, ½ cup vegan mayonnaise, and ½ cup Vegan Sour Cream. To use as a dressing for salad, stir in ¼ cup soymilk to thin. Refrigerate at least 1 hour before using.
3. Store in an airtight container and use within 5 days.

Sweet and Tangy Bacon Dressing

MAKES 2¼ CUPS

- 2 teaspoons oil
- ¼ onion, chopped
- ¼ cup vegan bacon bits
- ¼ cup sugar
- ¼ cup apple cider vinegar
- ¼ cup water
- 2 cups vegan mayonnaise

Your Savory Twice-Baked Potato (see "Comfort Food Meets Takeout") is begging for this! Don't let it down!

1. In a medium sauté pan over medium-high heat, sauté onions in oil until they turn golden and are very soft, about 10 minutes. Add the bacon bits and stir.
2. Stir in sugar, vinegar, and water, and bring to a boil, stirring constantly. Cook until sugar is melted and mixture boils for 2 full minutes. Remove from heat and cool before the next step.
3. In a medium bowl, whisk the cooled onion mixture with the mayonnaise until completely combined. Refrigerate.

Caesar Salad Dressing

While not an authentic Caesar, this has all the right elements of tang, creaminess, and garlic flavor with a hint of cheese from the nutritional yeast. (Plus, who really likes sardines, anyhow?)

1. Drain almonds and put in a food processor with lemon juice, mayonnaise, and oil. Process while adding water a tablespoon at a time until mixture is wet enough to process into a creamy salad dressing consistency.
2. Add nutritional yeast, garlic, salt, and pepper. Process until smooth.
3. Store in an airtight container and use within 4 days.

MAKES 1½ CUPS

1 cup raw almonds, soaked overnight
¼ cup lemon juice
¼ cup vegan mayonnaise
3 tablespoons olive oil
¼ cup water
1 tablespoon nutritional yeast
2 cloves garlic
1 teaspoon salt
½ teaspoon vegan Worcestershire sauce
½ teaspoon pepper

Garlic Chive Dip

You may want to plan on chowing down on this when you don't have to talk to anyone important afterward . . . your breath is likely to be a wee bit smelly. (Totally worth it.)

1. In a small bowl, combine the sour cream, chives, parsley, garlic, celery salt, onion, and pepper; mix until well combined. Refrigerate overnight.
2. Use within 4 days.

MAKES 1½ CUPS

1½ cups Vegan Sour Cream (see recipe in this chapter)
1 tablespoon fresh chives, minced
1 tablespoon fresh parsley, minced
2 cloves garlic, minced
1 teaspoon celery salt
1 teaspoon dried minced onion
½ teaspoon pepper

Green Chili Dip

MAKES ABOUT 2 CUPS

- ½ cup vegan mayonnaise
- 1 8-ounce container vegan cream cheese
- 1 4-ounce can diced green chilies
- 1 4-ounce can diced jalapeño
- 1 teaspoon garlic salt
- 2 tablespoons lemon juice
- ½ teaspoon pepper

I learned this recipe from the family I babysat for as a teen and it's gone through many incarnations over the years until finally going vegan. It is the absolute best served with a big bowl of Fritos.

1. Combine all ingredients with whisk until smooth. Refrigerate for a few hours before serving.
2. Store in the refrigerator and use within 4 days.

Chipotle Bean Dip

MAKES ABOUT 2 CUPS

- 2–3 whole chipotle chilies in adobo sauce
- 1 teaspoon oil
- ½ small onion, chopped
- ½ teaspoon salt
- ½ teaspoon cumin
- 1 15-ounce can black beans, drained and rinsed
- 1 cup Vegan Sour Cream (see recipe in this chapter)
- ¼ cup chopped cilantro
- Juice of 1 lime

Here's a complex bean dip that probably fits in better on the menu at a hip restaurant than it does in a book glorifying junk food, but you can dress it up or dress it down according to your needs. Pair with pita chips—or tortilla chips.

1. Put chilies in food processor and process until they becomes a paste.
2. In a nonstick pan, heat oil and sauté onion until translucent. Add salt and cumin to the pan and cook until the spice becomes aromatic, about 20 seconds.
3. Add the onion mixture and beans to the food processor and process until smooth.
4. Add Vegan Sour Cream, cilantro, and lime, and process until combined.
5. Store in the refrigerator and use within 4 days.

Basic Hummus

In my house, we always have a batch of homemade hummus in the fridge, because you just never know when a craving for creamy Mediterranean goodness will strike. It takes all of 6 minutes to make, so it's no hassle to keep us stocked. If you're unfamiliar with tahini, it's a roasted sesame-seed paste normally found with the international foods at the market. Be sure to stir really well before you use it.

1. In a food processor, combine garbanzo beans, water, oil, tahini, lemon juice, and salt. Process until very smooth, about 4 minutes.
2. Add-ins: garlic, jalapeño, roasted eggplant, roasted red peppers, paprika, toasted pine nuts, cilantro, basil, or chipotle peppers.
3. Store in an airtight container in the refrigerator and use within 4 days.

MAKES 2 CUPS

- 1 15-ounce can garbanzo beans, drained and rinsed
- 3 tablespoons water
- 3 tablespoons olive oil
- 3 teaspoons tahini
- 2 tablespoons fresh lemon juice
- 1 teaspoon salt

Pizza Hummus

No time to make an actual pizza? Take the quickest route to satisfy your urge with this cheesy tomato-y spread.

1. Combine all ingredients except pepperoni in a food processor and process until very smooth, adding a few tablespoons more water if needed to help blend. Spoon into a serving bowl and stir in pepperoni.
2. Serve with toasted pita or chunks of French bread.
3. Store in an airtight container in the refrigerator and use within 4 days.

MAKES 2 CUPS

- 1 3-ounce package sun-dried tomatoes
- 1 15-ounce can garbanzo beans, drained and rinsed
- ½ cup nutritional yeast
- ¼ cup olive oil
- 2 tablespoons lemon juice
- 2 cloves garlic
- 1 teaspoon basil
- 1 teaspoon oregano
- ½ teaspoon parsley
- ½ teaspoon salt
- 2 tablespoons water
- 1 4-ounce package Smart Deli Pepperoni slices, chopped

Spinach Artichoke Dip

SERVES 6

- 1 10-ounce package frozen spinach, thawed, drained, and chopped
- 1 14-ounce can artichoke hearts, drained and chopped
- 1 cup vegan mayonnaise
- 1 8-ounce container vegan cream cheese
- ½ cup Vegan Sour Cream (see recipe in this chapter)
- ¼ cup nutritional yeast
- ½ teaspoon garlic powder
- ½ teaspoon onion powder
- 1 teaspoon salt
- ½ teaspoon pepper
- ⅛ teaspoon cayenne pepper
- 1 cup vegan mozzarella shreds

There's a reason no one wants to move away from this stuff at a party. It's ridiculously rich and creamy! Be sure to serve while piping hot for yummiest results.

1. Preheat oven to 350°F. Mix all ingredients except mozzarella shreds in a 2-quart casserole dish. Top with mozzarella.
2. Bake for 20-25 minutes or until bubbly and just starting to brown.
3. Serve with French bread pieces or tortilla chips. Surely, there won't be leftovers. . . .

Lentil Walnut Pâté

This recipe may seem highbrow, but it's more about decadence. Splurge on some of the most buttery vegan crackers you can get your hands on, set out a plate of high-quality olives, and revel in the indulgence of it all!

1. Place walnuts in a sauté pan and toast over medium heat. Walnuts are done when they just begin to turn golden and smell fragrant. Remove from pan and set aside.
2. In the same pan, heat olive oil over medium-high heat and add onion and garlic. Cook for about 10-15 minutes, stirring occasionally, allowing onions to caramelize.
3. Place walnuts, onion-garlic mixture, lentils, soy sauce, and balsamic vinegar into a food processor. Process until mostly smooth, adding the ½ cup water a few tablespoons at a time until mixture can process freely.
4. Serve on a plate with a drizzle of olive oil on top and an assortment of crackers.

SERVES 6

- 1 cup raw walnuts
- 1 large onion, chopped
- 1 clove garlic
- 1 tablespoon olive oil
- 1 cup brown lentils, cooked in a quart of water for 40 minutes, drained
- 2 teaspoons soy sauce
- 1 teaspoon balsamic vinegar
- ½ cup water

Hot Fudge Sauce

MAKES ABOUT 1 CUP

½ cup vegan margarine
½ cup sugar
¾ cup cocoa powder
⅔ cup soy creamer
1 teaspoon vanilla

When any old chocolate won't do, turn to this. It's equally delicious eaten warm and melty over a bowl of coconut ice cream or cold mixed into a soygurt smoothie. Get creative!

1. In a medium saucepan over medium-high heat, melt margarine and add sugar, cocoa powder, and soy creamer, stirring constantly. Boil for 1 minute.
2. Remove from heat and stir in vanilla. Sauce will thicken upon cooling and can be reheated.
3. Store in an airtight container in the refrigerator and use within 2 weeks.

Caramel Sauce

MAKES ABOUT 1 CUP

¼ cup sugar
¾ cup packed brown sugar
½ cup soy creamer
¼ cup vegan margarine
1 teaspoon vanilla

Think beyond ice cream with this buttery-sweet sauce. (It really begs to be paired with a big bowl of crisp, sliced apples.)

1. In a medium saucepan over medium-high heat, stir sugar, brown sugar, creamer, and margarine with a whisk.
2. Bring to a full boil and continue cooking, stirring constantly, for 1 minute.
3. Remove from heat. Stir in vanilla. Sauce will thicken as it cools and can be reheated.
4. Store in an airtight container in the refrigerator and use within 2 weeks.

Tipsy Caramel Sauce

Sweet and thick with a hint of bourbon, this spiked version marries nicely with breakfast stuffs (think pancakes or waffles), although I've been known to dip cookies into it!

1. In a large saucepan over medium-high heat, bring the soy creamer, margarine, brown sugar, and salt to a full boil, whisking constantly. Turn heat down to medium-low and continue to whisk and cook until sauce begins to thicken. Remove from heat and stir in the bourbon.
2. Serve warmed on vegan ice cream or on top of apple pie. Refrigerate leftovers.

MAKES 1 CUP

½ cup soy creamer
½ cup vegan margarine
1 cup brown sugar
1 teaspoon salt
1 tablespoon bourbon

Pumpkin Pie Dip

Why be locked into an actual pie to enjoy pumpkin pie flavor? This way, you can eat the filling in whatever manner and with whichever vehicle you so desire—gingersnaps, graham crackers, pear slices, spoons, fingers . . . maybe it should be called Pumpkin Freedom Dip!

1. With a mixer or by hand, beat the powdered sugar into the cream cheese until smooth.
2. Stir in pumpkin, vanilla, cinnamon, ginger, nutmeg, and clove until completely mixed. Refrigerate overnight.

MAKES 2 CUPS

2 8-ounce containers vegan cream cheese
1 cup powdered sugar
1 15-ounce can pumpkin purée
1 teaspoon vanilla
1 teaspoon cinnamon
¼ teaspoon ground ginger
¼ teaspoon nutmeg
¼ teaspoon clove

Chocolate Chip Cookie Dough Dip

SERVES 6

1 8-ounce container vegan
  cream cheese
¼ cup vegan margarine
¼ cup coconut oil, softened
1 cup powdered sugar
¼ cup brown sugar
1 teaspoon vanilla
½ teaspoon salt
1 cup vegan chocolate chips
1 cup walnuts, chopped

Because we *all* know the dough is the best part of chocolate chip cookies.

1. In a stand mixer or by hand, beat cream cheese, margarine, and coconut oil until fluffy.
2. Mix in powdered sugar, brown sugar, vanilla, salt, chocolate chips, and walnuts until combined.
3. Serve with graham crackers.

CHAPTER 7

Savory Treats

With a Touch of
Sugar and Spice

Pretzel Bars

SERVES 6

1 cup brown sugar

½ cup vegan margarine

1 teaspoon salt

1½ cups crushed pretzels

½ cup peanuts or almonds, chopped

¼ cup vegan chocolate chips

Salty, sweet, and crunchy! Consider yourself forewarned: These disappear fast.

1. Grease an 8" × 8" baking dish.
2. In a small saucepan over medium-high heat, bring brown sugar, margarine, and salt to a boil. Boil for 4 minutes. Remove from heat.
3. In a medium bowl, stir pretzels and peanuts together. Pour on brown sugar mixture.
4. Press into prepared baking dish.
5. While hot, press chocolate chips into the top and spread evenly after they melt. Let cool completely before cutting into squares.

Mexicali Fondue

SERVES 4–6

1 tablespoon oil

¾ cup Soyrizo (about 6 ounces)

1 red bell pepper, diced

3 tablespoons flour

2 cups nondairy milk

2 cups vegan Cheddar shreds

¼ cup nutritional yeast

Tortilla chips

Soyrizo is a vegan version of traditional chorizo, which is a spicy sausage that hails from Spain but is also very popular in Mexico. Several manufacturers offer Soyrizo, so shop around to see which has the spiciness you desire. If you can't stand the heat, you may want to steer clear of this dip.

1. Preheat oven to broil. Lightly grease a 1-quart baking dish.
2. In a medium sauté pan over medium-high heat, sauté Soyrizo and red pepper in oil. Cook until red pepper is tender, about 5 minutes.
3. Using a whisk, stir flour into Soyrizo mixture and cook for 1 minute.
4. Add milk, stirring constantly until mixture boils and thickens. Add nutritional yeast and 1 cup vegan cheese.
5. Pour into prepared baking dish. Top with remaining cheese.
6. Place under broiler and bake for about 5 minutes or until top is golden.
7. Serve with tortilla chips.

Cheesy Popcorn

If you like Smartfood popcorn, you'll like this even better. But don't bother making it if you don't have nutritional yeast—it's the magical ingredient that turns this cheesy.

1. In a large stockpot with a lid, heat oil over medium-high heat, with a few kernels of popcorn in it. When those kernels pop, remove pot from heat, pour in the rest of the corn, and put the lid on. Warming all the kernels ensures that most will pop.
2. Wait about 30 seconds. Return pot to heat and shake pan as kernels begin to pop. When the popping slows to just one or two pops, remove from heat.
3. In a large bowl, toss hot popcorn with nutritional yeast, salt, and mustard powder.

SERVES 4

½ cup corn kernels
2 tablespoons oil
½ cup nutritional yeast
1 teaspoon salt
½ teaspoon mustard powder

Cheesy and Spicy Roasted Chickpeas

Nutty, crunchy yumminess is what you have here. Better start buying garbanzo beans in bulk because these tasty snacks are truly addictive!

1. Preheat oven to 350°F. Line a baking sheet with parchment paper.
2. In a large bowl, toss together garbanzo beans, olive oil, nutritional yeast, chili powder, and cumin.
3. Pour out onto prepared cookie sheet.
4. Bake for 20-25 minutes, stirring about halfway through.

SERVES 4

1 15-ounce can garbanzo beans, drained and rinsed
1 tablespoon olive oil
¼ cup nutritional yeast
1 teaspoon chili powder
½ teaspoon cumin

Baked Curried Sweet Potato Fries

SERVES 2

1 large sweet potato, peeled and cut into thin sticks

1 tablespoon olive oil

1 tablespoon curry powder, spicy or mild

1 teaspoon salt

½ teaspoon coriander powder

I adore sweet potatoes and eat them no fewer than four times a week, no joke. But I've never had a batch of sweet potato fries while eating out that meet my high expectations the way these do. The potatoes bake up soft inside, crisp outside, and you get a fragrant hint of curry. Man, are these good!

1. Preheat oven to 375°F. Line a baking sheet with lightly oiled parchment paper.
2. In a medium bowl, toss potatoes with olive oil, curry powder, salt, and coriander powder. Arrange in a single layer on prepared baking sheet.
3. Bake for 35 minutes, turning halfway through cooking.

Chocolate-Covered Potato Chips

SERVES 2

1 12-ounce bag chocolate chips

1 teaspoon coconut oil

About 20 ruffled potato chips

Vegan sprinkles (optional)

½ cup coconut (optional)

¼ cup pecans, chopped (optional)

The combo of crunchy potato chips plus melted chocolate yields a sinful result that belongs in the Junk Food Hall of Fame. (If only there was such a place. . . .)

1. Line a baking sheet with parchment paper.
2. In a small saucepan over medium heat, melt chocolate chips and coconut oil, stirring constantly, and remove from heat when most but not all chips are melted. Continue stirring until smooth.
3. Being careful not to break potato chip, place one chip at a time in chocolate and using two forks, turn chip in chocolate and lift, allowing excess chocolate to drip off. Place each chip on prepared baking sheet. Alternatively dip only half of chip into chocolate. Dip in sprinkles, coconut, or nuts (if using) while chocolate is still melted.
4. Allow to cool on baking sheet until chocolate is set. Speed up process by refrigerating for 5 minutes.

Microwave Sea Salt and Vinegar Chips

Yep, you can pop these babies in the microwave and nuke for a mere 3 minutes and you're well on your way to noshing. **Not too shabby.**

1. In a medium bowl, toss potatoes, olive oil, vinegar, and sea salt until evenly coated.
2. Line microwave-safe plate with parchment paper.
3. In small batches, arrange potatoes in a single layer on plate.
4. Microwave uncovered for 3-5 minutes, turning with tongs halfway through. Cooking time will depend on your microwave. Look for even browning. Remove from microwave; chips will crisp as they cool.

SERVES 2

1 large potato peeled, sliced paper-thin
1 tablespoon olive oil
1 tablespoon apple cider vinegar
1 teaspoon sea salt
½ teaspoon sugar

Cheesy Kale Chips

I'm sure you wouldn't believe me if I told you these kale chips actually have a flavor somewhat reminiscent of tortilla chips, so I think you should bake up a batch and see for yourself.

1. Preheat oven to 325°F. Line a baking sheet with parchment paper.
2. Remove stems and spines from kale and cut larger kale pieces in half.
3. In a large bowl, toss kale with oil, salt, nutritional yeast, and cayenne, using hands to rub seasoning into leaves.
4. Place in a single layer on prepared baking sheet; you might have to do this in batches, depending on the size of your bunch of kale.
5. Bake for 20 minutes, turning halfway through. Kale should be crisp but not brown.

SERVES 4

1 bunch kale, rinsed and dried
2 tablespoons oil
1 teaspoon salt
½ cup nutritional yeast
⅛ teaspoon cayenne pepper

Layered Pizza Dip

1 8-ounce container vegan cream cheese

1 3-ounce package sun-dried tomatoes, chopped

1 teaspoon oregano

1 cup marinara sauce

½ cup vegan pepperoni slices

¼ cup mushrooms, sliced thin

¼ cup bell peppers, sliced thin

¼ cup onions, sliced thin

1 cup vegan mozzarella shreds

French bread baguette

Perfect for when you can't be bothered with making dough for pizza, this warm, flavorful, multilayered dip (which feels more like a casserole) can be sopped up with big hunks of fresh French bread.

1. Preheat oven to 350°F. Lightly grease a 9" × 9" baking dish.
2. In a small bowl, mix cream cheese, sun-dried tomatoes, and oregano. Spread in the bottom of prepared dish. Top with marinara.
3. Layer pepperoni slices, mushrooms, bell peppers, and onions on marinara. Top with mozzarella cheese.
4. Bake for 20-25 minutes or until vegetables are tender and mozzarella is melted.
5. Serve with French bread torn into pieces.

Easy Candied Almonds

Crunchy, sweet, nutty, and FAST. You'll be chowing down in no time.

1. Line a cookie sheet with lightly greased foil.
2. In a small saucepan over medium-high heat, stir together brown sugar, margarine, and salt until sugar melts. Stir in almonds. Bring to a boil and reduce heat to medium.
3. Cook until mixture is golden. Remove from heat.
4. Pour onto prepared cookie sheet and allow to cool. Break into bite-sized pieces.

SERVES 4

½ cup brown sugar

3 tablespoons vegan margarine

½ teaspoon salt

1 cup raw almonds

Sweet and Spicy Nut Mix

In the mood for something hot and sweet? In this recipe, wasabi peas and cayenne provide the former and brown sugar provides the latter. It's an unbeatable combo!

1. Preheat oven to 350°F. In a medium bowl, combine brown sugar, corn syrup, melted margarine, salt, cinnamon, and cayenne. Add in nuts, pretzels, and wasabi peas. Stir to evenly coat.
2. Place nut mixture evenly spread out on a cookie sheet.
3. Bake for 10-15 minutes, stirring occasionally to break up clusters. Allow to cool completely.

SERVES 2–4

3 tablespoons packed brown sugar

1 tablespoon corn syrup

1 tablespoon vegan margarine, melted

1 teaspoon salt

½ teaspoon cinnamon

¼ teaspoon cayenne

1 cup raw nuts (almonds, peanuts, cashews, or any combination)

1 cup pretzels

½ cup wasabi peas

White Chocolate Potato Chip Clusters

SERVES 4

3 cups plain potato chips, crushed

½ cup peanuts, chopped

1 cup vegan white chocolate chips

If there's any dark or milk chocolate around, I almost always go for that over the white variety. That is, except when white chocolate is melted and mixed with crushed chips and peanuts, as they are in this brilliant recipe.

1. Line a cookie sheet with parchment paper.
2. In a medium bowl, toss together potato chips and peanuts.
3. In a small saucepan over medium heat, add white chocolate. Take chocolate off the heat while some chips are still melting and stir until smooth.
4. Pour melted chocolate over chips; toss with 2 spoons to coat chips and nuts.
5. Drop by the heaping tablespoonful onto prepared cookie sheet. Cool completely before eating.

Caramel Popcorn

SERVES 4

1 cup sugar

½ cup corn syrup

½ cup water

2 tablespoons vegan margarine

1 teaspoon vanilla

4 quarts popped popcorn

This honestly rivals the delicious stuff you can buy by the bucketload at the carnival. Perfect for the cravings that strike when the fair isn't in town.

1. Line a cookie sheet with foil and lightly grease it. In a medium saucepan over medium-high heat, stir together sugar, corn syrup, and water. Bring to a rapid boil, turn heat down to medium, and allow to cook for 10 minutes, watching for it to turn a golden color or to reach 300°F on a candy thermometer. Remove from heat.
2. Stir in margarine and vanilla; pour over popcorn and toss with 2 wooden spoons to coat evenly.
3. Place popcorn on prepared cookie sheet to cool.

CHAPTER 8

Cakewalk (Pies, Too)

Who Needs Butter?

Boston Cream Pie

SERVES 8–10

1 cup soymilk
1 tablespoon apple cider
   vinegar
2 cups self-rising flour
1 teaspoon baking soda
1 cup sugar
¼ cup applesauce
½ cup oil
1 teaspoon vanilla extract

Jersey diners have the market cornered when it comes to these awe-inspiring creations, but I dare you to find a diner that serves a vegan Boston cream pie. Here's how to recreate the original with dense sponge cake, a light and creamy whipped vanilla custard, and decadent chocolate ganache.

1. Preheat oven to 350°F. Grease and flour two round 8-inch cake pans.
2. In a small bowl, combine soymilk and vinegar; set aside for 5 minutes.
3. In a medium bowl, sift flour and baking soda.
4. In a small bowl, mix together sugar, applesauce, oil, and vanilla. Stir in soymilk mixture. Add to dry ingredients and mix well until smooth. Pour into prepared cake pans.
5. Bake for 25 minutes. Cool in pan.

Custard Filling

1. In a small bowl, whisk together soymilk and custard powder, then pour into a medium saucepan over medium heat. Bring to a boil, stirring constantly, and cook until mixture is very thick, about 5 minutes. When mixture becomes very stiff, remove from heat. Cool completely before next step.
2. In a stand mixer, beat margarine, sugar, and vanilla until very light and fluffy, about 5 minutes on high.
3. Add the custard mixture and 2 tablespoons soymilk to the beaten margarine and continue beating until they are completely incorporated and thick.
4. Place bottom layer of cake onto a cake plate. Spoon on custard. Top with second layer of cake.

2 cups soymilk
¼ cup custard powder
1 cup vegan margarine
1 cup sugar
1 teaspoon vanilla
2 tablespoons soymilk

Chocolate Ganache

1. Scald (bring to a boil) soymilk, remove from heat, add chocolate chips and margarine or oil, and stir until smooth.
2. Remove from heat. Allow to cool slightly.
3. Pour over cake when thick but still liquid. Refrigerate cake to allow ganache to set up and to keep custard firm.

½ cup soymilk
12 ounces chocolate chips
2 tablespoons vegan margarine or coconut oil

Rich Chocolate Cake with Ganache

2 cups soymilk

1 tablespoon apple cider vinegar

1¾ cups sugar

²/₃ cup vegetable oil

1½ teaspoons vanilla

2 cups flour

²/₃ cup cocoa powder

1½ teaspoons baking soda

1 teaspoon baking powder

½ teaspoon salt

If chocolate is your vice of choice, this cake will become a kitchen staple. It's moist, rich, and überchocolaty—and can be eaten completely alone.

1. Preheat over to 350°F. Grease and flour two 9-inch round cake pans.
2. In a small bowl, add the soymilk and vinegar; set aside for 5 minutes to thicken.
3. In a large bowl or mixer, stir together sugar, vegetable oil, and vanilla.
4. In a medium bowl, sift together flour, cocoa powder, baking soda, baking powder, and salt. If you do not have a sifter, a whisk works well to combine the dry ingredients.
5. Add the dry ingredients to the wet and stir by hand until very smooth or for 2 minutes using a mixer.
6. Divide batter evenly between greased and floured cake pans. Bake for 25 minutes or until a toothpick comes out mostly clean, checking often toward the end; do not overbake.
7. Allow to cool, then invert one layer onto a cake plate. Pour ganache over bottom layer, top with second layer, and pour ganache over top, allowing it to pour down the sides of cake. Refrigerate.

Chocolate Ganache

¹/₃ cup soymilk

12 ounces vegan chocolate chips

2 tablespoons sugar

1. Scald (bring to a boil) soymilk, remove from heat, add chocolate chips and sugar, and stir until smooth and sugar is melted.
2. Allow to cool slightly, stirring occasionally.
3. Pour over cake when thick but still pourable. Refrigerate cake to allow ganache to set up.

Chocolate Mint Cookie Layer Cake

For when Girl Scouts Thin Mints are just not in season, stock your pantry and you can enjoy the same awesome combo of chocolate and mint. The middle layer has a crunchy surprise brought on by the addition of Oreos! (Yep, they're vegan.)

SERVES 10–12

1 recipe Rich Chocolate Cake (see recipe in this chapter)
1 cup vegan margarine
4 cups powdered sugar
½ teaspoon mint extract
2 tablespoons nondairy milk
20 chocolate sandwich cookies, Oreos, 15 of them crushed

1. Bake cake as directed. Cool.
2. To make frosting, beat margarine in a stand mixer or by hand until light and fluffy. Stir in powdered sugar, mint extract, and milk, and continue to beat for 4 minutes.
3. Spoon ⅓ of the frosting into a medium bowl and fold in crushed cookies.
4. Place one layer of cake on a cake plate. Top with cookie frosting mixture and spread evenly. Top with second layer of cake; use remaining frosting to cover top and sides of cake.

Mint Drizzle

½ cup vegan chocolate chips
½ teaspoon mint extract

1. In a small saucepan over low heat, melt the chocolate chips, stirring constantly, until most are melted. Remove from heat and stir until smooth. Stir in mint extract. Allow to cool slightly.
2. Drizzle chocolate over cake, making a crosshatch pattern on top and letting chocolate drip down sides.
3. Top cake with remaining cookies cut in half and stood on the cut end.

S'mores Cake with Marshmallow Frosting

SERVES 10–12

1 cup vegan semisweet chocolate chips

2 cups graham crackers, crushed into ½-inch pieces

1 cup vegan margarine

4 cups powdered sugar

2 tablespoons nondairy milk

1 10-ounce container Ricemellow Crème, vegan marshmallow cream

1 recipe Rich Chocolate Cake, baked in two 9-inch round cake pans (see recipe in this chapter)

We could also call this the "Campfire Cake," it so closely emulates the flavor and texture of the classic camping dessert. Make sure to seek out vegan marshmallow cream; traditional marshmallow contains gelatin—no good.

1. In a small saucepan over low heat, melt the chocolate chips, stirring constantly, and removing from heat when most chips are melted. Stir until smooth.
2. Line a cookie sheet with parchment paper. Scatter graham cracker pieces in a single layer. Pour melted chocolate over graham pieces, tossing to coat evenly. Refrigerate to set chocolate.
3. In a stand mixer or by hand, beat margarine until light and fluffy. Stir in powdered sugar and milk and continue to beat for 4 minutes.
4. With a wooden spoon, fold in Ricemellow Crème gently.
5. Place one layer of cake on a cake plate. Add about ⅓ of the frosting and spread evenly. Top with second layer of cake; use remaining frosting to cover top and sides of cake.
6. Remove chocolate-covered graham crackers from refrigerator and break up into bite-sized chunks. Pile this on top of cake. Keep refrigerated.

Root Beer Float Cupcakes

Why settle for grabbing a soda when you can have root beer in the form of a cake? Watch out: Too much root beer reduction may send you to the dentist!

MAKES 12 CUPCAKES

1 12-ounce can root beer plus 1 cup root beer
2 tablespoons ground flaxseeds
¼ cup water
1 cup vegan margarine
1½ cups sugar
2½ cups flour
2 teaspoons baking powder
1 teaspoon salt
1 tablespoon root beer reduction

1. In a medium saucepan over high heat, bring can of root beer to a boil. Reduce heat to medium and simmer, stirring occasionally. Root beer should reduce down until only 25 percent of liquid is left or until root beer reduction coats the back of a spoon, 25-30 minutes. Cool completely before using.
2. Preheat oven to 350°F. Line two 12-cup cupcake tins with paper liners.
3. In a small bowl, mix flaxseeds and water; set aside.
4. In a mixer, cream margarine and sugar until light and fluffy. Add 1 cup root beer and 1 tablespoon root beer reduction and mix well.
5. In a medium bowl, mix together flour, baking powder, and salt. Add to creamed margarine and mix until smooth.
6. Fill prepared cupcake tins ¾ full. Bake for 18 minutes. Cool completely.
7. Frost with Root Beer Frosting and drizzle extra root beer reduction on top.

Root Beer Frosting

1 cup vegan margarine
4 cups powdered sugar
2 tablespoons root beer reduction

1. Beat margarine until light and fluffy; add powdered sugar and root beer reduction. Continue to beat until very fluffy.

Banana Chocolate Chip Cupcakes with Ganache

MAKES 12 CUPCAKES

1 cup sugar

½ cup oil

4 ripe bananas, mashed

¼ cup nondairy milk

1 teaspoon vanilla

2 cups flour

1 teaspoon baking soda

1 teaspoon salt

1 cup vegan chocolate chips

1 banana, sliced

1 recipe Chocolate Ganache (see recipe in this chapter)

A fun and chocolaty twist on banana bread! And a great way to use up overripe fruit—they mash into the batter a whole lot easier.

1. Preheat oven to 350°F. Line a 12-cup muffin tin with paper liners or grease and flour well.
2. In a medium bowl, stir together sugar, oil, bananas, milk, and vanilla.
3. In separate bowl, sift together flour, baking soda, and salt. Add to the banana mixture and mix until smooth. Stir in chocolate chips.
4. Fill prepared muffin cups ¾ full.
5. Bake for 15-17 minutes or until cupcakes are golden and center springs back when lightly touched. Cool completely.
6. Place a banana slice on top of each cupcake; pour a heaping teaspoonful of ganache over banana. Let ganache set.

Black Forest Cupcakes

Rich and tart, these decadent treats deserve top billing in the vast world of vegan cupcakes. They feature a dense cake, a hint of brandy, fluffy white frosting, and a brilliant crown of cherries.

1. Preheat oven to 350°F. Line a 12-cup muffin tin with paper liners or grease and flour well. Fill prepared muffin cups ¾ full with Rich Chocolate Cake recipe.
2. Bake for 15-17 minutes or until cupcakes are golden and center springs back when lightly touched. Cool completely.
3. In a small bowl, whisk together ½ cup reserved cherry liquid, sugar, and cornstarch until cornstarch is dissolved.
4. In a medium saucepan over medium-high heat, stir cornstarch mixture until it comes to a boil and thickens. Stir in cherries and bring back to a simmer. Cook for 3 minutes longer. Remove from heat and stir in almond extract. Allow to cool.
5. In a stand mixer or by hand, beat shortening until very fluffy. Add in powdered sugar and 1 tablespoon of milk. Beat until light and fluffy, adding last tablespoon of milk if frosting is too stiff. Add vanilla.
6. Brush the tops of cupcakes with kirsch, frost each with a heaping tablespoonful of frosting and a teaspoonful of the cherry mixture.

MAKES 12 CUPCAKES

- 1 recipe Rich Chocolate Cake (see recipe in this chapter)
- 1 15-ounce can pitted sour cherries, drained, liquid reserved
- ½ cup sugar
- 2 tablespoons cornstarch
- ¼ teaspoon almond extract (if you don't have almond extract, substitute ½ teaspoon vanilla)
- ½ cup nonhydrogenated vegan shortening
- 5 cups powdered sugar
- 1–2 tablespoons nondairy milk
- 1 teaspoon vanilla
- 4 tablespoons kirsch brandy

White Chocolate Raspberry Cheesecake

SERVES 10–12

- 15 chocolate sandwich cookies, Oreos, crushed fine
- 4 tablespoons vegan margarine, softened
- 1 16-ounce container firm tofu, drained
- 2 8-ounce containers vegan cream cheese
- ¾ cup sugar
- ¼ cup oil
- 2 tablespoons lemon juice
- ½ teaspoon salt
- 1 teaspoon vanilla
- 1 cup vegan white chocolate chips
- ¼ cup raspberry jam

Your palate will feel like it's taken a trip to paradise after you bite into this awesome creation, courtesy of crushed Oreos, white chocolate, and a swirl of raspberry jam.

1. Preheat oven to 350°F. Lightly grease a 9-inch springform pan.
2. In a small bowl, mix cookie crumbs with margarine. Press into prepared pan.
3. Add tofu, cream cheese, sugar, oil, lemon juice, salt, and vanilla to a blender. Blend until very smooth, about 2 minutes.
4. In a small microwave-safe container, melt ½ cup white chocolate chips, cooking at 15-second intervals, stirring after each until chocolate is smooth.
5. In a large bowl, stir together blended ingredients, melted white chocolate, and ½ cup white chocolate chips.
6. Pour over cookie crust, reserving ½ cup of batter.
7. In a small bowl, mix reserved batter with raspberry jam.
8. Spoon raspberry batter on top of cheesecake in a random pattern. Using a butter knife, swirl lightly to marble top of cheesecake.
9. Bake for 45 minutes. Turn oven off, leaving cheesecake in oven without opening door for another 20 minutes. Remove from oven and cool on counter. Refrigerate overnight.

Piña Colada Cheesecake

Tofu adds structure to lots of vegan cheesecakes, and this coconut rum and pineapple-flavored variety is no exception. Indulge when you're feeling like a taste of the tropical.

SERVES 10–12

1½ cups pineapple juice
2 tablespoons cornstarch
1½ cups graham cracker crumbs
2 tablespoons sugar
4 tablespoons vegan margarine
8 ounces firm tofu
4 8-ounce containers cream cheese
1½ cups piña colada mixer (12 ounces)
2 tablespoons coconut rum

1. Preheat oven to 350°F. Lightly grease a 9-inch springform pan.
2. In a small saucepan over medium-high heat, bring 1¼ cups pineapple juice to a boil. Cook for about 10 minutes or until juice reduces by half. Stir cornstarch into ¼ cup pineapple juice and add to saucepan, stirring constantly until very thick, about 3-5 minutes. Remove from heat.
3. In a small bowl, mix graham cracker crumbs and sugar with margarine. Press into prepared pan.
4. Add tofu, cream cheese, sugar, piña colada mix, and rum to a blender, and blend until very smooth, about 2 minutes.
5. Pour over graham cracker crust, reserving ½ cup of batter.
6. In a small bowl, mix together thickened pineapple juice and reserved batter.
7. Spoon pineapple batter on top of cheesecake in a random pattern. Using a butter knife, swirl lightly to marble top of cheesecake.
8. Bake for 45 minutes. Turn oven off, leaving cheesecake in oven without opening door for another 20 minutes.
9. Remove from oven and cool on counter. Refrigerate overnight.

Lemony Blueberry Crisp

SERVES 6

5 cups fresh blueberries

2 teaspoons instant tapioca

2 tablespoons sugar

   Zest of two lemons

1 cup quick oats

1 cup plain bread crumbs

½ cup vegan margarine

½ cup brown sugar

½ cup slivered almonds

This comes together in a snap and cooks into a thickened pie with lots of lemony flavor and a crispy crunchy top. Try it alongside vegan ice cream for yummiest results.

1. Preheat oven to 350°F. Have ready a 9" × 13" baking pan.
2. In a large bowl, toss blueberries, tapioca, sugar, and lemon zest together. Pour into baking dish.
3. In a medium bowl, combine oats, bread crumbs, margarine, sugar, and almonds until margarine is incorporated and mixture is crumbly. Pour over blueberries.
4. Bake for 45 minutes or until crumbs are golden brown. Serve hot or cold.

Peach Schnapps Cobbler

Another easy-to-assemble dessert that highlights the sweet-tart goodness of tender, fresh peaches. When you're craving something with warm flavors—nutmeg, cinnamon, and a buttery crust—this is your go-to. When right out of the oven, pour soy creamer on top and gobble up (before you're forced to share!).

1. Preheat oven to 350°F. Put the margarine in a 9" × 13" baking dish and place in the oven.
2. In a small bowl, mix milk and vinegar; set aside for 5 minutes.
3. In a medium bowl, sift flour, sugar, baking powder, and salt. Stir in milk/vinegar mix and schnapps.
4. In another bowl, mix together peaches, sugar, tapioca, cinnamon, and nutmeg.
5. Pour batter over hot margarine and follow with peach mixture.
6. Bake for 25-30 minutes or until cake is golden and has pulled away from sides of pan. Serve warm.

SERVES 6

- 1 cup vegan margarine
- 1 cup nondairy milk
- 1 tablespoon vinegar
- 1 cup flour
- 1 cup sugar
- 1 teaspoon baking powder
- ½ teaspoon salt
- 2 tablespoons peach schnapps
- 5 cups peaches, peeled, pitted, and sliced (roughly 2 pounds)
- ¼ cup sugar
- 1 tablespoon instant tapioca
- ½ teaspoon cinnamon
- ¼ teaspoon nutmeg

Tapioca Rum Custard

2 cups nondairy milk

1/3 cup small tapioca pearls

2 tablespoons cornstarch

1/3 cup sugar

1 teaspoon vanilla

2 tablespoons rum

You could also use instant tapioca for this, but it's a lot pricier than buying the pearls. If you use the pearls, don't skip the soaking step or you'll have a crunchy custard. This tastes great warm or cold!

1. In a small bowl, soak the tapioca pearls in the milk for at least 1 hour. Overnight is best.
2. In a medium saucepan, whisk together soaked pearls and milk with cornstarch.
3. Turn heat to medium-high and bring to a boil, stirring occasionally. Turn down to medium-low and let cook for 20 minutes, stirring often.
4. Taste for doneness. Tapioca pearls should be translucent and soft. Remove from heat.
5. Stir in vanilla and rum. Cover with plastic and let sit on the counter for 10 minutes.

Coconut Crème Brûlée

Like traditional crème brûlée, but much more delicious with the addition of coconut—a vegan favorite that also happens to be healthy. Of course, here we corrupt it with copious amounts of sugar!

1. Preheat oven to broil. Lightly grease four ramekins.
2. In a medium saucepan off the heat, whisk together cornstarch and coconut milk until smooth. Add sugar and turn heat to medium-high; bring to a full boil, stirring constantly. Cook until mixture thickens. Remove from heat. Stir in vanilla and coconut flakes.
3. Fill prepared ramekins and sprinkle sugar on top of each.
4. Place under broiler. Cook until sugar melts and begins to turn a light caramel color.

SERVES 4

½ cup cornstarch
2½ cups coconut milk
½ cup sugar
1 teaspoon vanilla
2 tablespoons coconut flakes
2 tablespoons sugar

Hot Fudge Pudding Microwave Cake

SERVES 6–9

½ cup flour

¼ cup sugar

¼ cup vegan chocolate chips

2 tablespoons cocoa powder

1 teaspoon baking powder

½ teaspoon salt

½ cup nondairy milk

1 tablespoon virgin coconut oil, melted

1 tablespoon cocoa powder

1/3 cup sugar

1 cup boiling water

Delicious, easy, made in the microwave. Need I say more?

1. Lightly grease bottom only of a 9" x 9" baking dish.
2. In a medium bowl, combine flour, sugar, chocolate chips, cocoa powder, baking powder, and salt. Add milk and coconut oil; mix well. Pour into prepared pan.
3. Sprinkle cocoa powder and sugar over batter.
4. Carefully pour boiling water over cake mixture.
5. Microwave on high 6–8 minutes, depending on your microwave. Let sit for 2 minutes. There should be a cake layer with a liquid fudge layer underneath.

Sweet Pie Crust

This flaky crust for fruit or custard pies should move into your vegan baking recipe box, as you'll use it time and again to make your favorite junk food. Homemade *always* beats store-bought when it comes to crusts.

1. In a food processor with the blade fitting attached, pulse flour, sugar, salt, and shortening until mixture resembles coarse meal. Alternatively, used a pastry blender or two knives to cut shortening into flour.
2. Add water a tablespoon at a time until a spoonful of dough can be shaped into a ball that doesn't fall apart; do not overmix.
3. Divide dough in half, shape into a ball, and flatten into a disk. Wrap in plastic and refrigerate for at least 1 hour.

MAKES TWO 9-INCH PIE CRUSTS

- 3 cups flour
- 2 teaspoons sugar
- 1 teaspoon salt
- 1½ cups Spectrum nonhydrogenated shortening, chilled
- 1/3 cup iced water

Chocolate Peanut Butter Pudding Pie with Pretzel Crust

SERVES 6–8

1½ cups crushed pretzels

3 tablespoons sugar

½ cup vegan margarine, melted

2 cups vegan chocolate chips

2 cups nondairy milk

3 tablespoons cornstarch

¼ cup coconut oil

½ cup peanut butter

1 teaspoon salt

1/3 cup sugar

If you like Reese's peanut butter cups, this vegan alternative is even better! Unlike Reese's, this dense pie features a crunchy pretzel crust sure to satisfy your fiercest salty-sweet craving.

1. Preheat oven to 350°F.
2. In a small bowl, mix together crushed pretzels, sugar, and margarine. Press into a 9-inch pie pan.
3. Bake crust for 8-10 minutes.
4. Place chocolate chips into a large bowl.
5. In medium saucepan off the heat, whisk together milk and cornstarch. Turn heat to medium; add coconut oil, peanut butter, salt, and sugar. Stirring constantly, bring to a boil and allow to cook until very thick. Remove from heat.
6. Pour over chocolate chips and stir until chips are melted and filling is smooth.
7. Spoon into prepared crust and refrigerate for 2 hours.

Pumpkin Pie with Bourbon Praline Sauce

For when you can't decide between pumpkin and pecan pie, here's the best of both worlds. Not in the mood to make pie? Make the Bourbon Praline Sauce instead and pour over a scoop of vegan vanilla ice cream for an equally exciting dessert.

1. Preheat oven to 425°F. Roll crust out to fit into a 9-inch pie pan, trim any overhang, and crimp edges with a fork. Place on a cookie sheet.
2. In a food processor, blend tofu until very smooth. Add pumpkin, sugar, pumpkin pie spice, and bourbon. Process until very smooth.
3. Pour into prepared pie crust.
4. Bake for 10 minutes. Lower oven temperature to 350°F and bake for 45 more minutes.
5. Cool completely. Refrigerate for a few hours or overnight before cutting.

SERVES 6–8

- ½ recipe Sweet Pie Crust (see recipe in this chapter)
- 1 16-ounce package silken tofu
- 1 16-ounce can pure pumpkin
- 2/3 cup sugar
- 2 teaspoons pumpkin pie spice
- 1 tablespoon bourbon

Bourbon Praline Sauce

1. In a medium saucepan over medium-high heat, stir together margarine, soy creamer, and brown sugar. Bring to a boil and let cook until it thickens, stirring constantly, about 5 minutes. Remove from heat.
2. Stir in bourbon and pecans. Serve warm over pumpkin pie.

- ½ cup vegan margarine
- ½ cup vegan soy creamer
- 1 cup brown sugar
- ¼ cup bourbon
- 1 cup pecans, chopped

Pumpkin Gingersnap Ice Cream Pie

SERVES 6–8

30 vegan gingersnaps
2 cups pumpkin purée
1 cup sugar
1 teaspoon salt
2 teaspoons pumpkin pie spice
1 cup pecans, chopped
1 pint vegan vanilla ice cream, softened

Warming flavors in a cooling format—serve this when you want to surprise your guests with the contrast of flavors and textures. I like to serve this around Thanksgiving, but it hits the spot anytime of the year.

1. Line a 9-inch springform pan with about 10 gingersnaps.
2. In a large bowl, mix pumpkin, sugar, salt, pumpkin pie spice, pecans, and ice cream.
3. Spoon half of pumpkin mixture over gingersnaps. Add 10 more gingersnaps over pumpkin layer. Top with remaining pumpkin mixture. Crush remaining gingersnaps and press into top of pie.
4. Freeze for at least 3 hours before serving.

Pumpkin Apple Cake with Ginger Frosting

You're in store for layers and layers of warm, spicy goodness when you craft this cake. Apply the icing straight away once the cake comes from the oven so that you get a lovely gooey ginger glaze once it cools. Now that you know the trick, get baking!

1. Preheat oven to 350°F. Lightly grease a 9" × 13" baking dish.
2. In a large bowl, toss apples with 1 teaspoon of cinnamon and 1 tablespoon sugar. Line prepared baking dish with apples.
3. In a stand mixer or by hand, beat margarine and sugar until light and fluffy. Add applesauce, vanilla, and pumpkin, and mix to combine.
4. In a medium bowl, sift together flour, baking soda, cinnamon, clove, ginger, and salt. Add to pumpkin mixture and stir well, about 2 minutes. Stir in oats. Pour over apples. Smooth top with a spatula.
5. Bake for 35–40 minutes or until top springs back when lightly depressed.
6. While cake is baking, prepare icing. In a stand mixer or by hand, cream shortening until light and fluffy, then add powdered sugar, ginger, cardamom, clove, and milk. Beat until all ingredients are combined. Spoon over top as soon as the cake comes out of the oven.
7. Allow cake to cool for about 15 minutes. Serve warm.

SERVES 8–10

- 2 baking apples, cored and sliced thinly
- 1 teaspoon cinnamon
- 1 tablespoon sugar
- 1 cup vegan margarine
- 1 cup sugar
- 1 cup applesauce
- 1 teaspoon vanilla
- 1 15-ounce can pure pumpkin
- 2 cups white flour
- 1 teaspoon baking soda
- 1 teaspoon cinnamon
- 1 teaspoon ground clove
- 1 teaspoon ground ginger
- 1 teaspoon salt
- 2 cups oatmeal

Frosting
- ½ cup (nonhydrogenated) vegan shortening
- 4 cups powdered sugar
- 1 teaspoon ground ginger
- ½ teaspoon cardamom
- ½ teaspoon ground clove
- 2 tablespoons nondairy milk

Berry, Peach, or Pumpkin Hand Pies

MAKES 1 DOZEN MINI PIES

1 recipe Sweet Pie Crust (see recipe in this chapter)

2 tablespoons nondairy milk

2 tablespoons raw sugar

Sweet little pies to serve to kids or when you want to wow with presentation. Use fresh fruit to make the creations that much more special.

1. Preheat oven to 350°F. Line a cookie sheet with parchment paper.
2. Roll out pie crust one disk at a time, rolling into a large rectangle about ⅛-inch thick. With a knife or pizza cutter, square edges of dough, then cut into 3" × 4" rectangles.
3. Prepare one or more of the following fillings.
4. Place a heaping tablespoonful of filling in the center of one dough rectangle, wet edge of dough, cover with a second rectangle, and crimp edges of dough closed with a fork.
5. Place on prepared cookie sheet. Brush with milk and sprinkle with raw sugar.
6. Bake for 15-20 minutes or until edges are golden brown.

Berry

1. In a medium saucepan over medium heat, bring berries and sugar to a simmer; cook until sugar is melted, about 5 minutes.
2. Turn heat up to medium-high.
3. Combine cornstarch and sugar; add to saucepan.
4. Cook until it comes to a full boil and filling is clear and thick. Remove from heat.

2 cups ripe berries, blueberry, blackberry, or raspberry
½ cup sugar
2 tablespoons cornstarch
2 tablespoons water

Peach

1. In a medium saucepan over high heat, combine peaches, sugar, flour, cinnamon, nutmeg, lemon zest, and lemon juice, stirring constantly until it comes to a boil.
2. Turn heat to medium and simmer until mixture becomes thick.
3. Remove from heat.

2 cups peaches, peeled, pitted, and chopped
½ cup sugar
2 tablespoons flour
½ teaspoon cinnamon
¼ teaspoon nutmeg
1 teaspoon lemon zest
1 teaspoon lemon juice

Pumpkin

1. In a medium saucepan over medium-high heat, combine pumpkin, sugar, brown sugar, cornstarch, and salt, whisking quickly to incorporate cornstarch.
2. Bring to a boil and cook until very thick.
3. Remove from heat.

2 cups canned pure pumpkin purée
½ cup sugar
½ cup brown sugar
4 tablespoons cornstarch
1 teaspoon salt
1½ teaspoons pumpkin pie spice

Deep-Dish Apple Brown Sugar Pie

SERVES 6–8

1 recipe Sweet Pie Crust
 (see recipe in this chapter)

4 Granny Smith apples,
 peeled, cored, and sliced

¼ cup sugar

1 cup brown sugar

2 tablespoons vegan
 margarine, softened

3 tablespoons flour

1 teaspoon cinnamon

¼ teaspoon nutmeg, ground

2 tablespoons milk

1 tablespoon sugar

The brown sugar in this pie gives it a distinctly caramel flavor, perfect served with a dollop of coconut whipped topping or a scoop of vegan ice cream.

1. Preheat oven to 450°F. Roll out one disk of pie crust to fit a 9-inch deep-dish pie pan. Roll out second disk large enough to cover pie.
2. In a large bowl, combine apples, sugar, brown sugar, margarine, flour, cinnamon, and nutmeg; mix well.
3. Spoon into prepared crust. Top with pie dough, cut any excess, and crimp edge with a fork. Slice four 1-inch holes to vent pie. Brush with milk and sprinkle with sugar.
4. Bake for 10 minutes. Turn oven down to 350°F and bake for an additional 45 minutes. Cool completely before cutting.
5. Serve with Coconut Whipped Cream (see recipe in this chapter).

Coconut Crust Banana Custard Pie

Reminiscent of diner banana cream pie, but with the addition of coconut! Custard powder could be a tough ingredient to find; try a grocery that carries imported foods as this is commonly used in the U.K. Made mainly of cornstarch, you could try substituting if you're really stuck.

SERVES 6–8

1½ cups coconut, toasted, plus 2 tablespoons for topping

½ cup graham cracker crumbs

2 tablespoons sugar plus 1 cup sugar

3 tablespoons vegan margarine, melted, plus 1 cup vegan margarine

1 cup soymilk plus 2 tablespoons soymilk

¼ cup custard powder

1 teaspoon vanilla

3 ripe bananas

1. Preheat oven to 350°F. Have ready a 9-inch pie plate.
2. In a medium bowl, combine coconut, graham cracker crumbs, 2 tablespoons sugar, and 3 tablespoons melted margarine; mix until well combined. Press into pie plate covering bottom and sides.
3. Bake for 10 minutes. Cool.
4. In a small bowl, whisk together 1 cup milk and custard powder. Pour into a medium saucepan over medium heat. Bring to a boil, stirring constantly, and cook until mixture is very thick, about 5 minutes. Cool completely before next step.
5. In a stand mixer, beat remaining margarine, remaining sugar, and vanilla until very light and fluffy, about 5 minutes on high.
6. Add the custard mixture and 2 tablespoons soymilk to the beaten margarine mixture and continue beating until they are completely incorporated, thick and smooth.
7. Slice bananas into bottom of prepared crust. Spoon custard over bananas and refrigerate overnight. Top with Coconut Whipped Cream right before you serve and sprinkle with coconut.

Coconut Whipped Cream

1 14-ounce can coconut milk (not lite; try Thai Kitchen)

2 tablespoons powdered sugar

1 tablespoon cornstarch

1. Refrigerate can of coconut milk overnight or put in freezer for 2 hours.
2. Open can and spoon out coconut milk solids, leaving liquid behind in can.
3. In a stand mixer or by hand, whip coconut solids, powdered sugar, and cornstarch for 5 minutes until fluffy.

Frozen Lemon Cream Pie

SERVES 6–8

1½ cups graham cracker
    crumbs

¼ cup sugar

4 tablespoons vegan
    margarine, melted

2 8-ounce containers vegan
    cream cheese

1¾ cups vegan Sweetened
    Condensed Milk

Zest of two lemons
(zest lemons before you
squeeze them)

Juice of two lemons

Sweet, tart, creamy, cool, and delicious! Any recipe that includes sweetened condensed milk automatically qualifies as junk food of the most delicious degree.

1. In a medium bowl, mix graham cracker crumbs, sugar, and margarine. Press into a 9-inch pie pan, covering bottom and sides.
2. In a mixer, beat cream cheese until fluffy, then add Sweetened Condensed Milk, lemon zest, and lemon juice, and mix thoroughly.
3. Pour over crust and freeze for 2 hours. If pie has been in the freezer overnight, let it thaw slightly before eating.

MAKES ABOUT 2 CUPS

4 cups soymilk

½ cup vegan margarine

2 cups sugar

1 teaspoon salt

Sweetened Condensed Milk

1. In a small saucepan, scald the soymilk; bring to a boil, turn heat down, and let simmer.
2. In a medium saucepan, melt the margarine and add the sugar and salt, stirring until the sugar is melted.
3. Add the milk to the margarine, slowly stirring constantly. Note the level of liquid in the pot; cook until it has reduced by half and the condensed milk is thick. Cool completely before using.

Candy and Cookie Fix

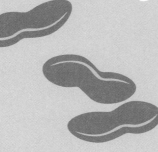

For the Ultimate Sweet Tooth

Chocolate Peanut Butter Wafer Candy Bar

MAKES 24 BARS

1 cup peanut butter

½ cup powdered sugar

¼ teaspoon salt

1 package vanilla wafer cookies*

1 12-ounce package vegan chocolate chips

1 teaspoon vegan margarine

Did you know it's incredibly easy to make candy bars? You can become master of your junk food kingdom when you create these ridiculously cravable bars that are made up of a crispy wafer and sweet peanut butter, smothered in a chocolate outer layer.

1. Combine peanut butter, sugar, and salt. Press a heaping teaspoonful on top of each wafer.
2. Place the chocolate chips and margarine in a microwavable bowl. Microwave in 15-second intervals, stirring after each until chocolate is melted through.
3. Working with two forks, dip each peanut butter-topped wafer into the melted chocolate and turn to coat. Place on wax paper until chocolate is set.

*NOTE: Gefen wafers are vegan and can be found in the kosher section of your local grocery store or online sources.

English Toffee

Buttery and crunchy—and better than the Brits can make!

1. Lightly grease an 11" × 7" × 2" baking dish.
2. In a medium saucepan over medium-high heat, bring sugar, margarine, 1 tablespoon of the almonds, and water to a boil, stirring constantly. Cook until a deep caramel color, about 15-20 minutes. Remove from heat, add vanilla, and pour into prepared baking dish.
3. Sprinkle chocolate chips over toffee and spread evenly when it begins to melt. Sprinkle almonds evenly over top of chocolate and gently press into chocolate layer.
4. Let harden for about 1 hour. Cut or break into pieces. Enjoy!

MAKES 1½ POUNDS

1 cup sugar
1 cup vegan margarine
3 teaspoons water
1 cup vegan semisweet chocolate chips
1 cup almonds, chopped
1 teaspoon vanilla

Coconut Almond Chocolate Candy Bar

MAKES 1 DOZEN BARS

1 cup sugar

¾ cup water

¼ teaspoon salt

1 8-ounce package unsweetened coconut

½ teaspoon vanilla extract

¼ teaspoon almond extract

½ cup whole almonds

2/3 cup vegan chocolate chips

If you love Almond Joy candy bars (which aren't vegan), give these babies a whirl. You will not be disappointed.

1. Lightly grease a cookie sheet.
2. In a large saucepan over high heat, bring sugar and water to a boil; cook until sugar is completely dissolved. Add salt and coconut to the pan. Lower heat to medium-high and continue to cook until the water has evaporated, about 10-15 minutes. Remove from heat. Stir in vanilla and almond extract.
3. Press the coconut mixture onto prepared sheet and press into a large square. While still warm, press an almond into the coconut about every 2 inches.
4. In a microwave-safe bowl, microwave the chocolate chips for 15 seconds at a time, stirring after each until melted and smooth. Pour evenly over coconut and almonds. Cool on the counter. Cut into bars.

Layered Crackers Candy Bars

Perfect for when a snack attack hits, the convenience store is closed, and all you have on hand is a box of saltines. In roughly an hour, you can have delicious candy bars!

1. Line an 8" × 8" baking dish with parchment paper.
2. Arrange half the saltine crackers in prepared baking dish.
3. In a large saucepan, combine graham cracker crumbs, sugar, margarine, and milk. Bring to a boil over medium-high heat and allow to boil for 5 minutes, stirring constantly. Remove from heat and stir in vanilla.
4. Pour over saltines. Top with remaining saltines.
5. In a microwave-safe bowl, microwave the chocolate chips and peanut butter for 15 seconds at a time, stirring between each until melted and smooth. Pour evenly over crackers. Refrigerate until set, about 1 hour. Cut into bars.

MAKES 1 DOZEN BARS

30 saltine crackers
½ cup graham cracker crumbs
1 cup packed brown sugar
½ cup vegan margarine
¼ cup nondairy milk
1 teaspoon vanilla
2/3 cup vegan chocolate chips
2 tablespoons peanut butter

Lime Cheesecake Truffles

1 8-ounce container of vegan
cream cheese

3¼ cups powdered sugar

Zest of two limes

3 tablespoons fresh lime juice

1 12-ounce bag vegan white
chocolate chips

1 teaspoon virgin coconut oil

½ cup graham cracker crumbs

1 tablespoon sugar

For when you're feeling a bit more refined, I present this truly unique white-chocolate truffle with a tart zing of lime and a sweet graham cracker coating.

1. In a mixer, combine cream cheese, sugar, lime zest, and lime juice; mix until completely combined. Refrigerate mixture until truffle mix is firm enough to form into balls, about 30 minutes.

2. Line a baking sheet with parchment paper. Using a melon baller or your hands, form truffle mix into 1-inch balls and place on prepared sheet. Refrigerate for 1 hour.

3. In a heavy-bottomed saucepan over medium heat, melt the white chocolate with the coconut oil, stirring until completely melted.

4. Place graham cracker crumbs and sugar in a shallow dish. Using two forks, dip each truffle into the chocolate and then place half of the coated truffle in crumbs; set on parchment sheet to set.

5. Keep truffles in the refrigerator.

Oreo Chocolate Truffles

You just can't go wrong with Oreos. It's a vegan junk food staple. Here I turn them into creamy truffles. Easy to make—and even easier to devour!

1. In a large bowl, combine cookie crumbs and cream cheese until very well combined. Refrigerate for at least 1 hour.
2. In a medium saucepan over medium-high heat, melt chocolate and coconut oil, stirring constantly until smooth. Remove from heat.
3. Shape crumb mixture into 1-inch balls.
4. Dip refrigerated balls into chocolate and place on parchment paper. Refrigerate until firm.

MAKES 2 DOZEN TRUFFLES

2 cups Oreos, crushed fine

1 8-ounce carton vegan cream cheese, softened

1 12-ounce package vegan chocolate chips

1 teaspoon coconut oil

Peanut Butter Truffles

MAKES 2 DOZEN TRUFFLES

- 1 cup chunky peanut butter
- 2 tablespoons vegan margarine
- 1 cup powdered sugar
- 1 12-ounce package vegan chocolate chips
- 1 tablespoon nonhydrogenated vegetable shortening
- 1½ cups chopped nuts, almonds, or pecans

Another vegan variation on the classic flavors of a Reese's, this time in truffle form for quick and simple inhalation! (These don't last very long in my house.)

1. Line a baking sheet with waxed paper.
2. Combine peanut butter, margarine, and powdered sugar, stirring until very smooth.
3. Roll into 1-inch balls. Place on prepared baking sheet.
4. Melt chocolate and shortening in a heavy saucepan over medium-low heat, stirring constantly. Using two forks, dip balls into chocolate, turning to cover on all sides. Roll in nuts and set truffles on prepared baking sheet to allow chocolate to set.
5. Refrigerate leftovers.

Peanut Butter Fudge

Peanut butter in all its delightful forms! Here you have an old-fashioned flavor and creamy fudgy texture. Make sure to cool completely before cutting or you'll end up with a ball of fudge instead of squares.

1. Lightly grease a 9" × 9" baking dish.
2. In a large saucepan over medium-high heat, bring sugar, brown sugar, soy creamer, corn syrup, and salt to a boil, stirring constantly. Once at a full boil, cover and cook for 1 minute.
3. Remove cover; do not stir. Continue cooking until a candy thermometer reaches 240°F. You can also test for this temperature by dropping a pea-sized amount of fudge into a glass of ice water; the fudge should easily form into a ball in the water and melt as you remove it from the water. Without stirring, spoon on peanut butter mixed with vanilla. Remove pan from heat and allow to cool on the counter for 20 minutes.
4. After 20 minutes, stir fudge with a wooden spoon until it begins to thicken and become creamy, about 2 or 3 minutes.
5. Spoon into prepared baking dish and smooth the top. Cool completely before cutting into squares.

MAKES 1 DOZEN SQUARES

1 cup sugar
1 cup packed brown sugar
½ cup soy creamer
2 tablespoons light corn syrup
½ teaspoon salt
1 teaspoon vanilla
¾ cup peanut butter

Vanilla Fudge

MAKES 1 DOZEN SQUARES

2½ cups sugar

¾ cup vegan sour cream

½ cup light corn syrup

3 tablespoons vegan margarine

1½ teaspoons vanilla

¾ cup walnuts, chopped

Did you know there are at least nine varieties of vanilla, each with distinct flavors, from places as far-flung as Papua New Guinea? If you really love the taste of vanilla, you may want to seek out something more exotic to try in this recipe, which yields a creamy fudge with a walnut crunch.

1. Lightly grease a 9" × 9" baking dish.
2. In a large saucepan over medium-high heat, bring sugar, sour cream, corn syrup, and margarine to a boil, stirring constantly. Once at a full boil, cover and cook for 1 minute.
3. Remove cover, do not stir. Continue cooking until a candy thermometer reaches 240°F. You can also test for this temperature by dropping a pea-sized amount of fudge into a glass of ice water; the fudge should easily form into a ball in the water and flatten as you remove it from the water. Remove pan from heat and allow to cool on the counter for 20 minutes.
4. After 20 minutes, stir fudge with a wooden spoon until it begins to thicken and become creamy, about 2 or 3 minutes. Stir in vanilla and walnuts.
5. Spoon into prepared baking dish and smooth the top. Cool completely before cutting into squares.

S'mores Squares

Who needs a campfire when you can make these from the comfort of your home? Familiar flavors in a familiar place set the stage for proper enjoyment of "junk."

1. Preheat oven to 350°F. Line a 9" × 9" baking dish with foil and lightly grease.
2. In a medium saucepan over medium-high heat, melt margarine. Remove from heat and add vanilla.
3. In a large bowl, mix graham cracker crumbs, sugar, marshmallows, and chocolate chips. Pour margarine over and mix well. Pour into prepared baking dish.
4. Bake for 15 minutes. Allow to cool completely. Use foil to remove bars from pan and cut into squares.

MAKES 2 DOZEN SQUARES

- ½ cup vegan margarine
- 1 teaspoon vanilla
- 1 cup graham cracker crumbs
- ¾ cup brown sugar
- 1 2.5-ounce bag vegan mini marshmallows
- 1 cup vegan semisweet chocolate chips

Scottish Shortbread Dipped in Chocolate

MAKES 1 DOZEN COOKIES

2 cups vegan margarine

1 cup sugar

4 cups flour

2 teaspoons vanilla

1 12-ounce package vegan chocolate chips

1 tablespoon coconut oil

Vaguely reminiscent of the ubiquitous NYC black and white cookies, here you've got a buttery, crunchy shortbread baked in a wedge, dipped in chocolate. Six ingredients and you're well on your way to noshing. . . .

1. Preheat oven to 275°F. Have ready an ungreased baking sheet.
2. In a mixer or by hand, cream margarine and sugar until light and fluffy. Add vanilla.
3. Add flour 1 cup at a time, mixing thoroughly after each addition.
4. On a floured surface, roll out cookie dough into a circle about ½-inch thick. Cut into wedges, place on cookie sheet, and prick with fork.
5. Bake for 45 minutes or until very lightly browned.
6. Line a baking sheet with parchment paper.
7. In a saucepan over medium-low heat, melt chocolate chips and coconut oil, stirring constantly. Cool slightly until chocolate is just warm to the touch. Holding the point of cookie, dip halfway into chocolate, allow excess chocolate to drip off. Place cookie on prepared baking sheet to set.

Red Velvet Whoopie Pies

Red velvet is all the rage these days, so why not take the popular cake and turn it into a whoopie pie? Because, really, when it comes down to it, all junk food should be portable.

1. Preheat oven to 400°F. Line a cookie sheet with parchment paper. In a small bowl, add the apple cider vinegar and flaxseeds to the soymilk, then set aside.
2. Using a mixer, cream margarine, sugar, and vanilla.
3. Sift together flour, cocoa, baking soda, and salt or use a whisk to combine the dry ingredients. Add the dry ingredients to the mixer. Add food coloring to the milk mixture and add to the mixer. Mix until smooth.
4. Drop by the heaping tablespoonful onto prepared cookie sheet, slightly flattening.
5. Bake for 8 minutes. Cool completely.

1 cup soymilk

1 tablespoon ground flaxseeds

1 tablespoon apple cider vinegar

2/3 cup vegan margarine

1 cup sugar

1 teaspoon vanilla

2¼ cups flour

¼ cup cocoa powder

1 teaspoon baking soda

1 teaspoon salt

2 tablespoons red food coloring, vegan-derived

Filling

1. Using a mixer, beat the sugar, shortening, margarine, cornstarch, and vanilla extract until light and fluffy.
2. For each whoopie pie, spread a tablespoon of frosting on one flattened side of cookie and sandwich it with another cookie, flat sides together.

2 cups powdered sugar

½ cup Spectrum nonhydrogenated shortening

2 tablespoons vegan margarine

1 tablespoon cornstarch

1 teaspoon vanilla extract

Chocolate Mint Whoopie Pies

MAKES 10 PIES

- 1 cup soymilk
- 1 tablespoon ground flaxseeds
- 1 tablespoon apple cider vinegar
- 2/3 cup vegan margarine
- 1 cup sugar
- 1 teaspoon vanilla
- 2¼ cups flour
- ¾ cup cocoa powder
- 1 teaspoon baking soda
- 1 teaspoon salt

- 2 cups powdered sugar
- ½ cups Spectrum nonhydrogenated shortening
- 2 tablespoons vegan margarine
- 1 tablespoon cornstarch
- 2 teaspoons mint extract

Chocolate outside, minty inside, pair alongside some vegan mint chocolate chip ice cream if you really want to get crazy.

1. Preheat oven to 400°F. Line a cookie sheet with parchment paper. In a small bowl, add the apple cider vinegar and flaxseeds to the soymilk, then set aside.
2. Using a mixer, cream margarine, sugar, and vanilla.
3. Sift together flour, cocoa, baking soda, and salt or use a whisk to combine the dry ingredients. Add the dry ingredients to the mixer and pour in milk mixture. Mix until smooth.
4. Drop by the heaping tablespoonful onto prepared cookie sheet, slightly flattening as you go.
5. Bake for 8 minutes. Cool completely.

Filling

1. Using a mixer, beat the sugar, shortening, margarine, cornstarch, and mint extract until light and fluffy.
2. For each whoopie pie, spread a tablespoon of frosting on one flattened side of cookie and sandwich it with another cookie, flat sides together.

Gingerbread Sandwich Cookies with Vanilla Cream

Terrifically flavorful spicy cookie with a creamy filling, this is like the adult version of an Oreo. Not that there's anything wrong with Oreos, but this will appeal to a more sophisticated palate. Don't omit the molasses; it's a key ingredient.

1. Line two baking sheets with parchment paper.
2. In a small bowl, mix together flaxseeds and water, then set aside.
3. Into a medium bowl, sift flour, baking soda, baking powder, ginger, cinnamon, and salt.
4. In a mixer, cream margarine, sugar, and molasses until fluffy. Add the flaxseed mixture and mix well. Add the dry ingredients and mix well.
5. Divide dough in half, shape each half into a log, and tamp edges on counter to make flat edges on each cylinder. Wrap in plastic and refrigerate for 1 hour.
6. Preheat oven to 350°F.
7. Unwrap log and cut with a sharp thin knife into ¼-inch rounds. Place 2 inches apart on prepared baking sheet.
8. Bake for 10-12 minutes. Slip cookies off the tray with parchment and cool.

Filling

1. In a stand mixer or by hand with a whisk, cream margarine until light and fluffy. Gradually add the powdered sugar until it is all incorporated. Add vanilla and beat for about 3 minutes.
2. Spoon about a tablespoon of filling between each pair of cookies.

MAKES 1 DOZEN COOKIES

- 2 tablespoons ground flaxseeds
- ¼ cup water
- 2 cups flour
- ½ teaspoon baking soda
- ½ teaspoon baking powder
- 1½ teaspoons ground ginger
- 1 teaspoon cinnamon
- ½ teaspoon salt
- ¾ cup vegan margarine
- ½ cup sugar
- ¼ cup molasses

- ½ cup vegan margarine
- 2 cups powdered sugar
- 2 teaspoons vanilla extract

Powdered Pecan Nugget Cookies

2 cups vegan margarine
¼ cup sugar
2 teaspoons vanilla
2 cups flour
1 cup pecans, chopped

Is it a ball? Is it a cookie? The debate rages on, although one thing's for sure: They belong in your belly!

1. Preheat oven to 350°F.
2. In a mixer, cream margarine and sugar until fluffy. Mix in vanilla.
3. Add flour and mix just to combine. Mix in pecans.
4. Form dough into walnut-sized balls and place 1 inch apart on an ungreased cookie sheet.
5. Bake for 15 minutes or until barely golden brown.
6. While still hot from the oven, roll in powdered sugar. Cool completely and roll in powdered sugar again.

No-Bake Orange Cookies

1 cup powdered sugar
1/3 cup frozen orange juice concentrate
¼ cup corn syrup
¼ cup vegan margarine
4 cups graham cracker crumbs
1 cup nuts

These taste like a baked cookie, citrusy and crispy, but you can give your oven a break.

1. In a large bowl, mix all ingredients until well blended.
2. Shape into 1-inch balls.
3. Store in an airtight container and use within 5 days.

Coconut Oatmeal Cookies

Some people are in the crisp camp when it comes to oatmeal cookies; others are in the chewy camp. Those in the latter will adore these, which are traditional but for the addition of coconut.

1. Preheat oven to 375°F. Lightly grease a cookie sheet.
2. In a large bowl, cream the margarine, brown sugar, and vanilla until fluffy. Add in applesauce and mix to combine.
3. Into a medium bowl, sift together salt, flour, baking powder, and baking soda. Add to the margarine mixture and mix well to combine. Stir in oats and coconut.
4. Shape into 1½-inch balls and place on prepared cookie sheet 2 inches apart. Slightly flatten with the bottom on a glass, dipped in sugar to prevent sticking.
5. Bake for 10 minutes or until just golden brown.

MAKES 2 DOZEN COOKIES

½ cup vegan margarine
1 cup brown sugar
1 teaspoon vanilla
¼ cup applesauce
½ teaspoon salt
1 cup flour
1 teaspoon baking powder
1 teaspoon baking soda
1¼ cups oats, old-fashioned
1½ cups coconut, unsweetened

Chocolate Chip Macadamia Nut Cookies

MAKES 2 DOZEN COOKIES

- 2 tablespoons ground flaxseeds
- ¼ cup water
- 1 cup plus 2 tablespoons vegan margarine
- 1 cup sugar
- 1 cup packed brown sugar
- 1 teaspoon vanilla
- 2½ cups flour
- 1½ teaspoons baking soda
- 1 teaspoon salt
- 1 12-ounce package vegan semisweet chocolate chips
- 1 cup macadamia nut halves

Get your ice-cold glass of soymilk ready for dunking when these come out of the oven piping hot and melty. So good!

1. Preheat oven to 350°F. Place a sheet of parchment paper on a cookie sheet.
2. In a small bowl, combine flaxseeds and water; set aside.
3. In a mixer, cream the margarine, sugar, and brown sugar until fluffy. Add vanilla. Mix in flaxseed-water mixture to combine.
4. In a medium bowl, sift together flour, baking soda, and salt. Add the flour mixture to the mixer until completely combined.
5. Drop cookies by the heaping tablespoonfuls onto an ungreased cookie sheet.
6. Bake for 8-10 minutes.

Sugar Cookies 2-Ways

Pick your pleasure: Make these with cookie-cutter shapes for a crisper cookie or use the log method for a chewier cookie.

1. In a small bowl, mix the milk and flaxseed; set aside.
2. In a mixer, beat the sugar and margarine until fluffy. Add the vanilla and flaxseed mixture and mix well.
3. In a medium bowl, sift flour, baking powder, and salt; add to mixer and mix until well combined.

For cookie-cutter cookies:

4. Divide the dough into thirds and flatten each into a disk. Wrap in plastic and refrigerate for at least 1 hour.
5. Preheat oven to 400°F. Lightly grease a cookie sheet or line with parchment paper.
6. Use one disk at a time, keeping the other disks refrigerated. Roll out dough on a floured surface or between sheets of plastic to ⅛-inch thickness. Use cookie cutters or a biscuit cutter to shape cookies. Place 2 inches apart on prepared cookie sheet.
7. Sprinkle with sugar before baking or leave plain for decorating with icing.

MAKES 2 DOZEN COOKIES

- 2 tablespoons ground flaxseeds
- ¼ cup nondairy milk
- 2 cups sugar
- ¾ cup vegan margarine
- 1 teaspoon vanilla extract
- 3 cups plus 2 tablespoons flour
- 2 teaspoons baking powder
- ½ teaspoon salt
- ½ cup sugar

Potato Chip Cookies

MAKES 2 DOZEN COOKIES

1 cup brown sugar

1 cup white sugar

1 cup nonhydrogenated vegan shortening

4 tablespoons vegan margarine, softened

1 teaspoon vanilla

2¼ cups flour

1 teaspoon baking soda

3 cups potato chips, crushed

½ cup peanuts, chopped

1 tablespoon sugar

If you thought potato chips were merely meant to be chomped on straight from the bag or dunked in dip, think again. We're getting creative, folks! Here, I fold them, along with peanuts, into a cookie.

1. Preheat oven to 350°F. Line a cookie sheet with parchment paper.
2. In a stand mixer or by hand, beat brown sugar, white sugar, shortening, and margarine until fluffy, about 5 minutes. Mix in vanilla.
3. In a small bowl, sift flour and baking soda. Add to margarine mixture and mix until well combined. Stir in 2 cups crushed potato chips and peanuts.
4. In a small bowl, stir together remaining crushed chips and sugar.
5. Using a heaping tablespoonful of dough, roll each cookie into a ball and press the bottom only into the potato chip-sugar mixture. Place on prepared baking sheet, chip-covered side down.
6. Bake for 10-12 minutes or until just light golden brown.

Cinnamon Roll Cookies

With these luscious little treats, it's all about the icing. Enjoy for breakfast (or anytime, really)!

1. Use one disk of cookie dough at a time, leaving the other refrigerated. Roll dough into an approximately 12" × 5" rectangle on a floured surface or between layers of plastic wrap.
2. In a small bowl, combine margarine, brown sugar, and cinnamon. Spread half of this mixture onto cookie dough rectangle. Roll into a long log. Wrap in plastic; repeat with the rest of cookie dough and filling. Refrigerate logs for at least 1 hour.
3. Preheat oven to 350°F. Line a baking sheet with lightly greased parchment paper.
4. Using a thin sharp knife, cut dough into ½-inch slices and place on prepared cookie sheet.
5. Bake for 10 minutes or until light golden brown. Allow to cool for 2 minutes on the cookie sheet, then transfer to a wire rack to cool completely.

Icing

1. Beat the cream cheese and powdered sugar together, adding milk 1 tablespoon at a time until frosting is thick but pourable.
2. Drizzle over cooled cookies.

MAKES 2 DOZEN COOKIES

1 recipe Sugar Cookies 2-Ways dough (see recipe in this chapter), divided into two disks and refrigerated for 1 hour
½ cup vegan margarine
½ cup Sucanat or organic brown sugar
2 teaspoons cinnamon

1 8-ounce container vegan cream cheese
¾ cup powdered sugar
4 tablespoons nondairy milk

Rugelach

MAKES 2 DOZEN COOKIES

1 cup vegan margarine

1 8-ounce carton vegan cream cheese

1 cup flour

½ cup apricot jam

1/3 cup sugar

½ cup walnuts, finely chopped

1 tablespoon cinnamon

Here it is. The classic deli cookie, demystified. Feel free to sub out the apricot jam with any kind of jam that you're craving.

1. In a large bowl, mix margarine, cream cheese, and flour. Divide into four balls, wrap with plastic, and refrigerate for 2 hours.
2. Preheat oven to 375°F. Line a cookie sheet with parchment paper.
3. On a floured surface, roll each ball into a 10-inch diameter circle. With a knife, cut each circle into 10 or 12 wedges. On each wedge, spread jam evenly in a thin layer.
4. In a small bowl, mix sugar, walnuts, and cinnamon. Sprinkle over jam on each wedge.
5. Roll gently from the wide part of wedge to the point. Place on prepared baking sheet. Sprinkle with any remaining cinnamon-sugar mixture.
6. Bake for 35 minutes or until golden brown.

Butterfinger Chunk Cookies

In this recipe, you make your own Butterfinger chunks, then bake them into a totally decadent cookie. A quick Google search should turn up vendors who carry Chick-O-Stick candy, but expect to have it shipped, as it's not available everywhere.

1. Line a baking sheet with parchment paper.
2. In a saucepan over medium-high heat, melt the chocolate and coconut oil, stirring constantly until smooth. Remove from heat. Stir in Chick-O-Stick candy and mix to coat all pieces. Pour out onto prepared baking sheet. Refrigerate until chocolate is set. Break up into small pieces.
3. Preheat oven to 350°F. Line another baking sheet with parchment paper.
4. In a small bowl, mix flaxseeds and water; set aside.
5. In a stand mixer or by hand, cream margarine, sugar, brown sugar, and vanilla until light and fluffy. Stir in flaxseed mixture. Mix in flour and baking soda until dough forms. Stir in candy pieces.
6. Form cookies into 2-inch balls and place 2 inches apart on prepared cookie sheet.
7. Bake for 10-12 minutes or until edges are light golden brown. Let cool on cookie sheet for 2 minutes, then transfer to a wire rack to cool.

MAKES 1 DOZEN COOKIES

- 1 cup vegan chocolate chips
- 1 tablespoon coconut oil
- 2 cups Chick-O-Stick candy, broken into marble-sized chunks
- 1 tablespoon ground flaxseeds
- ¼ cup water
- 1 cup vegan margarine
- ½ cup sugar
- ½ cup packed brown sugar
- 1 teaspoon vanilla
- 2 cups all-purpose flour
- 1 teaspoon baking soda

CHAPTER 10

Grab 'n' Go Sweets

Sinful Bars, Brownies, and More

Hawaiian Pineapple Coconut Bars

MAKES 12–14 BARS

1 20-ounce can pineapple chunks, drained and chopped
4 tablespoons cornstarch
½ cup sugar
½ cup vegan margarine, melted
2 cups brown sugar
2 cups coconut, flaked
2 cups flour
1 teaspoon salt

When you enjoy these bars while wearing a lei, it increases the flavor exponentially! You know, really get in the spirit.

1. Preheat oven to 350°F. Line a 9" × 13" baking dish with parchment paper.
2. In a medium saucepan, combine pineapple, cornstarch, and sugar. Cook, stirring constantly, until mixture becomes thick; remove from heat.
3. In a medium bowl, mix margarine and brown sugar. Add coconut, flour, and salt; mix until well combined.
4. Press half of crumb mixture into prepared baking dish.
5. Bake for 10 minutes.
6. Spread pineapple evenly over crust. Crumble the remainder of dough over pineapple and press lightly.
7. Bake for 30 minutes or until top is golden brown. Cool completely before cutting into bars.

Almond Joy Bar Cake

Dense like a brownie, this cake is great for when you feel like a nut. Candy bar craving, solved.

1. Preheat oven to 350°F. Lightly grease a 9" × 13" baking dish.
2. In a small bowl, mix flaxseeds and water; set aside.
3. In a mixer, cream margarine, almond extract, and sugar until light and fluffy. Add flaxseed mixture and mix.
4. Sift together flour, cocoa powder, baking powder, and salt. Add to the creamed margarine mixture.
5. Pour half of batter into prepared baking dish and top with coconut and ¾ cup chopped almonds. Pour in the other half of batter. Sprinkle with remaining almonds.
6. Bake for 30 minutes. Cool completely before cutting.

SERVES 12

- 2 tablespoons flaxseeds, ground
- ¼ cup water
- ¾ cup vegan margarine
- 1 teaspoon almond extract
- 2 cups sugar
- 1¼ cups flour
- ½ cup cocoa powder
- 1 teaspoon baking powder
- 1 teaspoon salt
- 1½ cups flaked coconut
- 1 cup almonds, chopped

Blueberry Crumble Bars

MAKES 8-10 BARS

- 1 tablespoon ground flaxseeds
- ¼ cup water
- 3¼ cups flour
- 1 cup sugar
- 1 teaspoon baking powder
- 1 cup vegan margarine
- 4 cups fresh blueberries or blackberries
- 1 teaspoon lemon zest
- ½ cup sugar
- 1 tablespoon cornstarch

Don't let the ample amount of fresh berries in this dish fool you; with 1 cup of sugar and 1 cup of margarine, it's still full-on junk food.

1. Preheat oven to 350°F. Line a 9" × 13" baking pan with foil, lightly greased.
2. In a small bowl, combine flaxseeds and water; set aside.
3. In a mixer or by hand, combine flour, 1 cup sugar, baking powder, and margarine until evenly combined and crumbly.
4. Press half the crumble mixture into prepared pan.
5. In a medium bowl, mix together the berries, lemon zest, sugar, and cornstarch. Spoon on top of crust. Top with the remainder of crumble mixture.
6. Bake for 40-45 minutes or until crumble is lightly browned.
7. Cool completely. Use foil to lift crumble out of pan and cut into bars.

Pecan Pie Bars

A portable version of the perennial holiday favorite. If you're feeling extra junky, melt some vegan chocolate chips to drizzle over the top of this before it is set out to cool. Yum!

1. Preheat oven to 350°F. Lightly grease a 9" × 9" baking dish.
2. In a medium bowl using a whisk or a fork, combine flour, 2 tablespoons brown sugar, and margarine until a dough forms. Press into prepared baking dish.
3. Bake for 15 minutes.
4. In a medium bowl, mix ½ cup brown sugar, applesauce, corn syrup, pecans, melted margarine, vanilla, and salt. Pour this mixture over crust.
5. Bake for 25 minutes or until edges are light golden brown. Cool completely before cutting into bars.

MAKES 8–10 BARS

11/3 cups flour
2 tablespoons brown sugar
1 cup vegan margarine, melted and divided
½ cup brown sugar
¼ cup applesauce
½ cup light corn syrup
½ cup pecans, finely chopped
1 tablespoon coconut oil
1 teaspoon vanilla
½ teaspoon salt

Peanut Butter Cup Cookie Bars

MAKES 8–10 BARS

1½ cups finely crushed peanut
    butter sandwich cookies
    (such as Nutter Butters)

¼ cup vegan margarine,
    melted

¼ cup coconut oil, melted

1 cup peanut butter

1½ cups powdered sugar

¼ cup coconut oil, melted

2 tablespoons vegan
    margarine, melted

1 12-ounce bag vegan
    semisweet chocolate chips

½ cup peanut butter

Yet another pairing of two of the most revered flavors in the junk food universe: chocolate and peanut butter. In this case, you get a peanut butter cookie crust, followed by a thick peanut butter layer topped with chocolate. A total Reese's ripoff!

1. Line a 9" × 9" baking dish with parchment paper or waxed paper.
2. For crust, in a medium bowl, combine the crushed cookies, margarine, and ¼ cup coconut oil. Press into prepared dish.
3. For the filling, in the same bowl, combine 1 cup peanut butter, powdered sugar, ¼ cup coconut oil, and 2 tablespoons margarine, stirring until smooth. Spoon onto crust, patting evenly to distribute. Refrigerate for 30 minutes.
4. In a small saucepan over medium-low heat, melt the chocolate chips with ½ cup peanut butter, stirring constantly.
5. Pour over filling layer and refrigerate until set enough to cut into bars.

No-Bake Chocolate Chunk Banana Peanut Balls

Got four ingredients? How about four minutes? Then you could have a terrific snack with virtually no effort. . . .

1. Mix graham crackers, banana, peanut butter, and chocolate chips until thoroughly combined.
2. Shape into 1½-inch balls.

MAKES 12 BALLS

2 cups graham cracker crumbs
1 banana, mashed
½ cup chunky peanut butter
½ cup vegan chocolate chips

PB&J Bars

Be careful if you have kids, because once you make these cookies—a sugar cookie with strawberry filling and a peanut butter crumble—they'll never go back to eating regular PB&J sandwiches again. (Consider yourself warned.)

1. Preheat oven to 375°F. Line a 9" × 9" baking dish with foil and lightly grease.
2. Press two-thirds of the sugar cookie dough into prepared pan. Spread with jam, leaving a ¼-inch border along the edges free of jam.
3. In a medium bowl, mix the peanut butter and powdered sugar until completely combined. Add the remainder of the cookie dough and granola mix. Crumble this mixture over jam layer.
4. Bake for 25-30 minutes or until topping turns golden brown. Cool completely. Use foil to lift from pan and cut into bars.

MAKES 10–12 BARS

1 recipe Sugar Cookies 2-Ways dough (see recipe in "Candy and Cookie Fix")
2/3 cup strawberry jam
½ cup granola cereal
¾ cup peanut butter
¼ cup powdered sugar

Real-Deal Baklava

MAKES 2 DOZEN BARS

3 1/3 cups chopped nuts
(almonds, walnuts,
pistachios, or a combination
of each)

1 cup sugar

1 teaspoon ground cinnamon

1 pound frozen phyllo
dough (check for vegan
ingredients, or look for
The Fillo Factory brand),
defrosted and covered with
a damp towel

1 cup vegan margarine,
melted

Phyllo dough, which is the essence of this traditional dessert with cinnamon, nutty syrup-soaked layers, can be easily made from scratch, but you can save time by buying it prepared. Just be sure to check the ingredients to make sure they're not sneaking in any animal products.

1. Preheat oven to 350°F. Lightly grease a 9" × 13" baking dish.
2. In a medium bowl, mix the nuts, 1 cup sugar, and cinnamon.
3. Using kitchen shears, cut the entire stack of phyllo dough in half so that the sheets fit in the baking dish.
4. Lay one sheet of phyllo in the baking dish and brush with melted margarine; keep the stack of waiting dough covered as you work. Repeat 6 times. Spoon about 3 tablespoons of the nut mixture in an even layer. Top the nut mixture with two sheets of phyllo, then nut mixture. Repeat two layers of margarine-brushed dough and nuts until you run out of nuts. The last layers will be about five or six layers of margarine-brushed phyllo.
5. Using a very sharp knife, cut through the layers of dough in a diamond pattern almost but not quite down to the bottom of dough layers.
6. Bake for 50 minutes. Remove from oven.

Sugar Syrup

1 cup water

1 cup sugar

½ cup agave

2 tablespoons lemon juice

1. While the baklava is baking, place water, sugar, agave, and lemon juice in a saucepan; bring to a boil, stirring to dissolve the sugar. Once it reaches a boil, turn the heat down to medium-low and simmer for about 20 minutes. Allow syrup to cool completely before the next step.
2. When the baklava comes out of the oven, evenly pour Sugar Syrup over the baklava. Allow to cool completely.

Hazelnut Chocolate Baklava

This tastes like a marriage of baklava and Nutella. The latter isn't vegan, so this should satisfy your chocolate-hazelnut craving, lickety-split.

1. Preheat oven to 350°F. Lightly grease a 9" × 13" baking dish.
2. While the baklava is baking, place 1 cup water, sugar, agave, and lemon juice in a saucepan; bring to a boil, stirring to dissolve the sugar. Once it reaches a boil, turn the heat down to medium-low and simmer for about 20 minutes. Allow syrup to cool completely before the next step.
3. In a medium bowl, mix the nuts, sugar, and chocolate chips.
4. Using kitchen shears, cut the entire stack of phyllo dough in half so that the sheets fit in the baking dish.
5. Lay one sheet of phyllo in the baking dish and brush with melted margarine; keep the stack of waiting dough covered as you work. Repeat 6 times. Spoon about 3 tablespoons of the nut mixture in an even layer. Top the nut mixture with two sheets of phyllo, then nut mixture. Repeat two layers of margarine-brushed dough and nuts until you run out of nuts. The last layers will be about five or six layers of margarine-brushed phyllo.
6. Using a very sharp knife, cut through the layers of dough in a diamond pattern almost but not quite down to the bottom of dough layers.
7. Bake for 50 minutes. Remove from oven.
8. When the baklava comes out of the oven, evenly pour Sugar Syrup (See recipe for Real-Deal Baklava) over the dish. Allow to cool completely.

MAKES 2 DOZEN BARS

1 cup water
1 cup sugar
½ cup agave
1 tablespoon lemon juice
31/3 cups chopped hazelnuts
1 cup packed brown sugar
1 cup vegan semisweet chocolate chips
1 pound frozen phyllo dough (check for vegan ingredients or try The Fillo Factory brand), defrosted and covered with a damp towel
1 cup vegan margarine, melted

S'mores Chocolate Chip Cookie Bars

MAKES 10–12 BARS

2 tablespoons ground flaxseeds

¼ cup water

1 cup plus 2 tablespoons vegan margarine

1 cup sugar

1 cup packed brown sugar

1 teaspoon vanilla

2½ cups flour

1½ teaspoons baking soda

1 teaspoon salt

½ cup graham crackers, broken into 1-inch pieces

½ cup vegan semisweet chocolate chips

1 2-ounce package vegan mini marshmallows

Like a blondie with a s'mores topping, bars like these bake up fast and are best enjoyed while the marshmallows are still totally melty.

1. Preheat oven to 350°F. Lightly grease a 9" × 9" baking dish.
2. In a small bowl, combine ground flaxseeds and water; set aside.
3. In a mixer, cream the margarine, sugar, and brown sugar until fluffy. Add vanilla. Mix in flaxseed mixture.
4. In a medium bowl, sift together flour, baking soda, and salt. Add the flour mixture to the margarine mixture and stir until completely combined.
5. Spoon dough into prepared pan and smooth top. Sprinkle with graham cracker pieces, chocolate chips, and marshmallows. Press into dough lightly.
6. Bake for 30 minutes or until edges are golden brown and center is set.

Pumpkin Shortbread Bars

The ultimate melding of three different desserts: shortbread, pumpkin pie, and a crumble. Make sure to let these set before cutting, that is, if you want to keep them neat. If you plan on eating straight from the pan, more power to you.

1. Preheat oven to 350°F. Press Scottish Shortbread dough into a 9" × 13" baking dish. Bake for 12 minutes.
2. In a mixer or by hand, beat pumpkin, milk, ½ cup brown sugar, cornstarch, and pie spice until very well combined. Pour over crust.
3. In a large bowl, combine oats, flour, brown sugar, pecans, baking soda, and margarine.
4. Crumble on top of filling.
5. Bake for 25-30 minutes or until top is golden brown.
6. Cool completely before cutting; for best results, refrigerate overnight before cutting.

MAKES 12–14 BARS

- 1 recipe Scottish Shortbread, prepared but not baked (see "Candy and Cookie Fix")
- 1 16-ounce can pumpkin purée (pure pumpkin)
- 2/3 cup nondairy milk
- ½ cup packed brown sugar
- 4 tablespoons cornstarch
- 1 tablespoon pumpkin pie spice
- ½ cup oats
- ¼ cup flour
- ¼ cup packed brown sugar
- ¼ cup chopped pecans
- ½ teaspoon baking soda
- ¼ cup vegan margarine, melted

Maple Pecan Shortbread Bars

MAKES 12–14 BARS

1 recipe Scottish Shortbread,
   unbaked (see "Candy and
   Cookie Fix")
2 cups coconut flakes
1 cup pecans, chopped
1 cup pure maple syrup
1 teaspoon salt

Make like you're traveling to Vermont or Canada when you enjoy these maple goodies.

1. Preheat oven to 350°F. Line a 9" × 13" baking dish with parchment paper.
2. Press the Scottish Shortbread dough into prepared pan.
3. Bake for 20-25 minutes or until very lightly brown at edges.
4. In a medium saucepan over medium-high heat, mix coconut, pecans, syrup, and salt. Cook, stirring constantly, until liquid is absorbed by the coconut.
5. Spoon over crust, spreading evenly.
6. Bake for about 10 minutes or until coconut becomes golden. Cut while still warm. Cool completely before removing from pan.

White Chocolate Raspberry Bars

This bakes in two stages but is deceivingly simple to make. Surprise a loved one who has a special sweet tooth for white chocolate with these rich, crunchy-fruity bars.

1. Heat oven to 350°F. Grease a 9" × 9" baking dish.
2. In a mixer, combine sugar, margarine, vanilla, and salt until completely combined. Add flour and mix until it resembles coarse crumbs. Set aside 1 cup of crumb mixture.
3. Heat half of the white chocolate in a saucepan over low heat just until melted. Add applesauce and melted white chocolate to the remaining crumb mixture and mix until a dough forms. Press into prepared baking dish.
4. Bake for 12 minutes.
5. Pour raspberry jam over crust and spread to within a ¼ inch of the edge. Sprinkle white chocolate chips over jam. Top with reserved cup of crumbs.
6. Bake for 25 minutes. Cool completely before cutting.

MAKES 8–10 BARS

- 1 cup sugar
- 1 cup vegan margarine
- 1 teaspoon vanilla
- 1 teaspoon salt
- 2½ cups flour
- 1 12-ounce package vegan white chocolate chips
- ½ cup applesauce
- 1 cup raspberry jam

Coconut Cherry Vodka Bars

MAKES 12–14 BARS

1½ cups coconut flakes
½ cup dried cherries
½ cup vanilla vodka
1 cup flour
½ cup vegan margarine
¼ cup sugar
2 tablespoons ground flaxseeds
2/3 cup sugar
1 teaspoon vanilla
½ cup water
¼ cup flour
1 teaspoon baking powder
½ teaspoon salt
¼ cup almonds, chopped

If you don't have vanilla vodka on hand, you can always steep a vanilla bean in the vodka to infuse the flavor. Do this at least 2 hours before you plan to bake, longer if you're able. The result is a coconut-cherry-vanilla-vodka filling baked into a buttery-crisp bar.

1. In a small bowl, combine coconut, dried cherries, and vanilla vodka; steep for 1 hour.
2. Preheat oven to 350°F. Line a 9" × 9" baking dish with parchment paper.
3. In a medium bowl, combine 1 cup flour, margarine, and sugar until well blended. Press into bottom of prepared baking dish.
4. Bake for 20 minutes.
5. In a medium bowl, mix ground flaxseeds, sugar, vanilla, and water, and stir well. Add the ¼ cup flour, baking powder, and salt, mixing until well combined.
6. Drain vodka from cherries and coconut; shake in a colander to remove moisture.
7. Stir coconut, cherries, and nuts into flour mixture. Pour over baked crust.
8. Bake for 30-35 minutes or until golden brown.

No-Bake Peanut Butter Cup Bars

Peanut butter plus chocolate, the no-bake version!

1. Line a 9" × 9" baking dish with parchment paper or waxed paper.
2. For crust, in a medium bowl, combine the crushed cookies, ¼ cup margarine, and ¼ cup coconut oil. Press into prepared dish.
3. For the filling, in the same bowl, combine 1 cup peanut butter, powdered sugar, ¼ cup coconut oil, and 2 tablespoons margarine, stirring until smooth. Spoon onto crust, patting evenly to distribute. Refrigerate for 30 minutes.
4. In a small saucepan over medium-low heat, melt the chocolate chips with ½ cup peanut butter, stirring constantly. Pour over filling layer and refrigerate until set enough to cut into bars.

MAKES 8–10 BARS

- 1½ cups finely crushed vegan peanut butter sandwich cookies (such as Nutter Butter Bites)
- ¼ cup vegan margarine, melted, plus 2 tablespoons vegan margarine, melted
- ¼ cup coconut oil, melted, plus ¼ cup coconut oil, melted
- 1 cup peanut butter plus ½ cup peanut butter
- 1½ cups powdered sugar
- 1 12-ounce bag vegan semisweet chocolate chips

No-Bake Blueberry Cheesecake Bars

MAKES 12 BARS

- 2 cups graham cracker crumbs
- ½ cup almonds, ground
- 2 tablespoons sugar
- ¼ cup vegan margarine, melted
- 2 8-ounce containers vegan cream cheese
- 2 tablespoons sugar
- 1 tablespoon lemon zest
- 1 tablespoon lemon juice
- ½ teaspoon salt
- 2 cups blueberries

Lemon, blueberries, and almonds seem healthy enough, but then add the cream cheese, graham crackers, sugar, and margarine, and this goes squarely into the junk food category. No muss or fuss with these tangy-sweet bars.

1. Line a 9" × 9" baking dish with parchment paper, slightly overlapping edges to make it easier to remove bars from dish.
2. In a medium bowl, combine graham cracker crumbs, almonds, 2 tablespoons sugar, and margarine until well combined. Press into prepared baking dish.
3. In a stand mixer or by hand, beat cream cheese, 2 tablespoons sugar, lemon zest, lemon juice, and salt. Pour over crust, spreading evenly. Top with blueberries.
4. Refrigerate for at least 4 hours or overnight. Cut into bars.

No-Bake Oatmeal Almond Butter Bars

An oat drop cookie held together with a caramel almond butter mixture—perfect for when you forgot to bake something but committed to bringing dessert!

1. Line a cookie sheet with parchment paper. Lightly grease an 8" × 8" baking dish.
2. In a large saucepan over high heat, bring sugar, milk, and margarine to a boil; stir constantly for 2 minutes. Remove from heat. Stir in almond butter and vanilla.
3. Pour mixture over oats and mix well so that all the oats are coated.
4. Press into prepared baking dish. Set aside to firm, about 1 hour.

MAKE 8–10 BARS

- 2 cups sugar
- ¼ cup nondairy milk
- ½ cup vegan margarine
- ½ cup almond butter
- 1 teaspoon vanilla
- 3 cups quick oats, uncooked

No-Bake Brownie Bites

**MAKES 1 DOZEN
BROWNIE BITES**

1 cup cashews

½ cup almonds

1 cup dates

2 tablespoons coconut oil

¼ cup cocoa powder

1 teaspoon vanilla extract

½ cup coconut, grated, or ½ cup powdered sugar

Keep the oven off but break out the food processor to make these scrumptious bites. (Sometimes, simpler is junkier.)

1. In a food processor, process cashews and almonds until very finely chopped. Add dates, coconut oil, cocoa powder, and vanilla; process until very well blended.
2. Roll brownies in coconut or powdered sugar.

Chocolate Chunk Brownies

If you served these at a bake sale, you could easily charge double that of regular mix brownies. Duncan Hines just seems lame after you taste one of these chunky, nutty beauties.

1. Preheat oven to 350°F. Grease a 9" × 13" baking dish.
2. In a small bowl, mix soymilk and apple cider vinegar. Set aside for 5 minutes.
3. In a medium bowl, sift together flour, cocoa powder, baking soda, and salt.
4. Add sugar, oil, and vanilla to soymilk mixture; stir well. Add to dry ingredients and stir until smooth. Stir in chocolate and nuts. Pour into prepared baking dish.
5. Bake for 30-35 minutes.

MAKES ABOUT A DOZEN BROWNIES

- ¾ cup soymilk
- 1 tablespoon apple cider vinegar
- 2 cups flour
- ½ cup cocoa powder
- 1 teaspoon baking soda
- 1 teaspoon salt
- 1½ cups sugar
- ¾ cup oil
- 1 teaspoon vanilla
- 1 cup vegan semisweet chocolate chips
- ½ cup nuts (almonds or hazelnuts), roughly chopped

Mocha Cheesecake Brownies

MAKES ABOUT A DOZEN BROWNIES

¾ cup soymilk

1 tablespoon apple cider vinegar

2 cups flour

½ cup cocoa powder

1 teaspoon baking soda

1 teaspoon salt

1½ cups sugar

¾ cup oil

1 teaspoon vanilla

1 8-ounce container vegan cream cheese

½ cup powdered sugar

3 tablespoons strong black coffee

Imagine taking your morning mocha, a rich, creamy cheesecake, and fudgy brownies and putting them in a blender—that's what you've got here. Of course, not in terms of consistency, but the flavors meld in a way that's truly sublime.

1. Preheat oven to 350°F. Grease a 9" × 13" baking dish.
2. In a small bowl, mix soymilk and apple cider vinegar. Set aside for 5 minutes.
3. In a medium bowl, sift together flour, cocoa powder, baking soda, and salt.
4. Add sugar, oil, and vanilla to milk mixture and stir well. Add to dry ingredients and stir until smooth. Pour into prepared baking dish.
5. In a medium bowl, stir together cream cheese, sugar, and coffee until completely mixed. Drop by heaping tablespoonfuls onto brownie mix. Using a butter knife, swirl cheesecake gently into brownie batter.
6. Bake for 35-40 minutes.

Crispy Brownie Squares

Favor crisp over chewy? If so, this is the junk food for you: a brownie masquerading as a flat cookie bar topped with crunchy almonds.

1. Preheat oven to 400°F. Line two 8" × 8" baking dishes with lightly greased parchment paper, slightly overlapping to ease in lifting brownie out of pan later.
2. In a medium saucepan over medium-low heat, melt coconut oil with cocoa powder, stirring constantly until smooth. Remove from heat.
3. Stir in sugar, cornstarch, vanilla, salt, and flour until well blended.
4. Spread ½ cup of batter into each baking dish and sprinkle with nuts.
5. Bake for 12 minutes or until top is firm to the touch.
6. Cool for 4 minutes and then cut brownies into small squares. Cool completely in baking dish. Using parchment, lift brownies out of pans.

MAKES 12 SQUARES

¼ cup coconut oil
3 tablespoons cocoa powder
½ cup sugar
1 tablespoon cornstarch
1 teaspoon vanilla
½ teaspoon salt
¼ cup flour
1/3 cup almonds, finely chopped

White Chocolate Lemon Brownies

8 tablespoons vegan margarine

1 cup vegan white chocolate chips

½ cup brown sugar

Zest of three lemons

2 tablespoons lemon juice

¼ cup silken tofu, blended smooth

1¼ cups flour

1 cup vegan white chocolate chips

A white brownie! It's lemony with a smooth white-chocolate flavor and studded with more white chocolate chips. The addition of tofu makes it dense and moist.

1. Preheat oven to 325°F. Line a 9" × 9" baking dish with parchment.
2. In a large saucepan over medium-high heat, melt the margarine and 1 cup white chocolate chips, stirring constantly until smooth. Allow to cool until it is no longer hot, stirring occasionally. Add brown sugar, lemon zest, lemon juice, and tofu, stirring until well combined.
3. Stir in flour and 1 cup white chocolate chips.
4. Pour batter into prepared baking dish.
5. Bake for 40 minutes.
6. Allow to cool, then refrigerate overnight. Cut into bars.

Glazed Lemon Bread

Enjoy for breakfast, lunch, dinner, snack time, or anytime. The tart flavor is offset by the sweet glaze that melts into the bread when it's right out of the oven—delicious!

1. Preheat oven to 350°F. Grease and lightly flour a 9" × 5" loaf pan.
2. In a stand mixer or by hand, beat margarine, applesauce, sugar, lemon zest, and lemon juice until very well mixed.
3. Sift together flour, baking powder, and salt. Add to margarine mixture and stir just until combined; do not overmix.
4. Pour into prepared loaf pan.
5. Bake for 45-50 minutes or until a knife comes out clean.
6. Mix 2 tablespoons lemon juice with powdered sugar. When lemon bread is hot from the oven, drizzle with glaze. Cool completely before cutting.

MAKES 10–12 SERVINGS

- ½ cup vegan margarine
- ½ cup applesauce
- 1 cup sugar
- Zest of three lemons (zest lemons before juicing)
- 3 tablespoons lemon juice
- 1½ cups flour
- 1 teaspoon baking powder
- 1 teaspoon salt
- 2 tablespoons lemon juice
- ½ cup powdered sugar

Chocolate–Chocolate Chip Banana Bread

MAKES 10–12 SERVINGS

1¼ cups sugar

½ cup oil

1 tablespoon flaxseeds, ground

¼ cup applesauce

2 cups mashed banana

1 teaspoon vanilla extract

2 cups flour

¾ cup cocoa powder

1½ teaspoons baking soda

½ teaspoon salt

1 3-ounce chocolate bar, roughly chopped

A banana bread for chocolate lovers; a real junk-foodie take on the classic.

1. Preheat oven to 350°F. Lightly grease a 9" × 5" loaf pan.
2. In a large bowl, mix together sugar, oil, flaxseed, applesauce, banana, and vanilla.
3. Sift together flour, cocoa powder, baking soda, and salt. Add to the banana mixture and stir until just combined; do not overmix. Fold in chopped chocolate.
4. Pour into prepared loaf pan.
5. Bake for 50-60 minutes. Cool for 10 minutes, then transfer to a wire rack. Cool completely before slicing.

Peanut Butter Bread with Cream Cheese Frosting

Many people like to spread peanut butter on bread, but in this ingenious combo, you spread sweet cream cheese onto *peanut butter bread*. A nice twist, if you ask me.

1. Preheat oven to 350°F. Lightly grease a 9" × 5" loaf pan.
2. In a medium bowl, mix flour, baking powder, and salt.
3. In a small bowl, mix sugar, peanut butter, milk, and flaxseeds. Add to flour mixture and mix just until combined.
4. Pour into prepared loaf pan.
5. Bake for 50 minutes.
6. In a stand mixer or by hand, beat cream cheese until light and fluffy. Add powdered sugar and mix until combined, about 2 minutes. Spread onto warm cake and allow to cool completely.

MAKES 10–12 SERVINGS

- 2 cups flour
- 2 teaspoons baking powder
- ¼ teaspoon salt
- 1/3 cup sugar
- ¾ cup peanut butter, chunky
- 1 cup nondairy milk
- 2 tablespoons ground flaxseeds
- 1 8-ounce container vegan cream cheese
- 1½ cups powdered sugar

Index

About the Author

Lane Gold is a vegan chef in Los Angeles, where she grew up. Her catering co-op features seasonal, organic, and local foods, taking full advantage of the excellent agricultural resources of Southern California. When she isn't in a kitchen, you can find her leading the charge on bringing food justice issues to the fore, volunteering at local farms, or in her backyard tending her garden.